HIGH ODYSSEY

To Alison
I hope this inspires you
to visit Colorado and
conquer the trails

Hax

HIGHWAY ODYSSEY

TRAVELING TO, OR RUNNING FROM

ALEXANDER FLINT

Outskirts Press, Inc.
Denver, Colorado

Preface

This effort had its origins many generations ago on another continent. It officially began in 1977 with my son's odyssey journal. I began to mold it into a book form in 1999 after my return from Salida, Colo. In creating it, I included family legends and some military experiences I had along the way.

In the chapter with the CIA operative, I did not use his real name. Regarding my Marine Corps buddies, I took the details of their heroic acts from public records. Concerning my mother's ancestors' names and dates, I tried to be as accurate as possible for future generations who may be interested in maintaining their family tree.

The incident of the sex pervert thrown to his death from a roof on Elizabeth Street was related to me in 1957 on my job as a wireman for the New York Telephone Company. My foreman used the incident as to illustrate to us to treat the female residents of Little Italy with respect.

Writing of the deaths of my parents was emotional for me and served as a catharsis. In addition, it demonstrates that life will end one day and it's better to leave positive feelings. The photo of Mom and Dad and I with the caption,

"We never lose what is filed away in our hearts," hangs in my dining room where it was taken in 2002. When I look at that picture I am reminded of the wonderful bond that my children, my parents and I shared. Both of them were both incredible individuals who touched so many people.

I dedicate this book to Mom and Dad.

Contents

CHAPTER 1

Rolling Memories

It was 1999 as I drove east, towards New York, backtracking on the same route I had taken three weeks ago. I was used to this drill; I had done it twenty times before. This was the twenty-first consecutive year I had spent my summer vacation in Colorado. As the miles on the odometer clicked on and the Colorado mountain landscape rolled passed, I began to reminisce. As in all my previous trips, I pondered the previous chapters of my life.

Some people despise long road trips. I relish them. I get a feeling of accomplishment from the car-seat meditation and it leaves me feeling content. As I left Chuck's ranch in Salida and wound my way through Trout Creek Pass, I put on a Willie Nelson CD and thought of the memorable events that occurred while here in the Rockies.

Chuck Jensen, a retired NY City Firefighter and former Staten Islander turned-rancher had settled in Salida, Colorado. Chuck was a Roy Rogers type hero who could have been a movie matinee idol. He bought a ranch in the early 1970s. He traded his fireboat boots for boots

In the Saddle on Bill

with spurs, bought a cowpony named Bill and a mountainside of cattle to breed and brand. He started the Ute Valley Ranch and created his own bona fide brand to slap on his calves.

Ute Valley Ranch

Chuck told me why he loved it so much out there. He spoke of the scent of nature; he particularly relished the fragrant air after an afternoon shower. He also pointed to the white water Arkansas River which formed the Eastern border of his property and the sounds of relaxation it created. Then, with great enthusiasm, he went on to explain that nowhere else on earth, (he was a navy veteran who had sailed around the world) did he ever see nighttime stars that existed at his 7,500 foot altitude log ranch house. He asked me, "Did you ever taste eggs like we had for breakfast?" "Not since I was a little boy," I replied. "You see," he proudly exclaimed, "Food even tastes better in this clean air."

One evening after dinner he took me for a walk to a distant barn on his property. He instructed me to climb the ladder against the wall and look in the loft window opening. Before I got fully situated to stick my head in, there was a rush of air, a flurry of feathers, and passing inches over my head flew a barn owl ready to begin a night's hunt. He indicated with pleasure that we were early enough for me get a look at his resident rodent destroyer.

Chuck was very happy in his Rocky Mountain home. He also liked the history of his land. Back home in his den that evening, he handed me a baseball sized cannon ball. He said his land was used by Zebulon Pike, the founder of the now famous peak. Pike used it as a refuge to spend the winter of 1833. There actually is an historical marker on State Highway 285, which borders the Western side of his ranch that explains in detail Pike's winter of 1833. The marker indicated that cannon were used to take buffalo for food so the US Army contingent could survive the winter.

Chuck, Bill and Me

Chuck is in cowboy heaven now, he died in 1994. He was 83, and I miss him.

At his memorial service, a young man named Peter gave this moving eulogy.

CHARLES WILLIAM JENSEN

I knew him as Bill. I'd heard him called Charles, Uncle Bill, Dad, Chuck, and Chief. I'd even called him a few spicier names when he and I had heated up a campfire with political and religious rhetoric. But, to me, he was just Bill. A simple man by his own reckoning. Of all the things I can say about him, the most telling is his belief that complexity was optional and for enjoyment only (like around the campfire). Right was right, wrong was wrong, and being a man was a very simple thing-hard sometimes, but simple. You got up, got dressed, and did the simple things that God had given you to do that day. This was important for me to hear and see a living example. My life was so incredibly complicated when I met Bill that every day was overwhelming to contemplate, much less to live. I could see both sides of every issue and would, sometimes, invent a third side. I could argue each side with equal ease, leaving me in complete disarray regarding and moral, ethical, or personal conviction. Bill saw one side clearly and could not possibly argue anything that he didn't believe. He had character and the courage of his convictions, and while I didn't always agree with his position, I always admired the fact that he had one. I remember trying to dislodge him from his convictions. I'd use all of the rhetorical and logical skills that I had, only to have him say, "Well it doesn't matter what you say-right is right, and I believe in that." It was very frustrating.

I have come to have my own set of convictions, today. They do not mirror Bill's necessarily, except that I, too, believe that right is right. I no longer live by situation ethics and have developed "character" and courage of my convictions. I owe him a debt for helping me find my way through all of that. Today, people see me as a sane, stabile, mature rock in a wildly changing world. That's exactly how I saw Bill in my bad old days. I came to know Bill in the late 1960's; those were the bad old days for me. I was a spiritually and emotionally bankrupt alcoholic who was trying to find a way to live without the only thing that had ever made life okay-alcohol. I was barely on this side of sanity (some would have argued about which side) and social acceptability. My sister, Faith, and Bill were inlaw'ed to each other and occasionally commiserated over their lots in marriage. Bill was living, at that time, in a camper outside the YMCA for which he was superintendent (or some such thing). I'd visit him and use the pool and other facilities with him in the off hours. We'd play cards in his camper and talk about life. But, most of all I remember camping and fishing.

I'm not sure how it started, but Bill would take me to

Lake Solitude in New Jersey. We'd spend the entire day on the lake with some junk food and soda pop. Then, we would cook dinner over the campfire and talk. It was in that environment that this loner and self-proclaimed outcast began to talk his way back into the human race. We would sometimes get so roaring angry that I'm sure we scared off the wildlife for miles around. Bill would take all the abuse that I could muster for the world and human race. I was forced to face my own self in the mirror that he provided. We had a great deal of fun, but it was marvelous therapy too.

Bill was my hero; he was my John Wayne. He had every virtue that a boy, wanting to be a man, could wish to have. He was big, bold, and brave. I know that he was, at times, small unsure, and afraid, but he believed that you shouldn't let them see you sweat. He had a man's job and functioned very well in a man's world. He was a man. He invested a lot of energy in helping me to understand that, although I felt like a boy, I could be a man. The man I am today is due to God's grace and my own acceptance of that responsibility. But, there if you look closely, you will see a faint outline left by Bill's guiding hand.

I wish I could share the memories I have of those summer and fall nights with Bill. Sometimes, when the campfire coals and our arguments had died down to flickering embers, we would have long periods of silence, just looking up at the stars. In southern New Jersey, the stars seemed to be more plentiful and brighter than anywhere else; certainly more so than the ever-mantled city nights. It was there that I learned the meaning of the word serenity – and for that, I will ever be grateful to the memory of my friend Bill.

I don't know the details of Bill's upbringing, but I know

he had known hard times and hard knocks. I suspect that the peace he found in later life was not easily won. By the time I knew him he had begun to fight less and enjoy more. He never liked to surrender, but he learned to find compromise and the middle ground. I, in turn, learned a lot about that from him. I learned that if I was willing to get in his face for something I really believed in, then he was usually willing to consider a new idea or at least acknowledge that there might be more than one answer. I learned to stand up, and I learned to listen.

Now, don't get the idea that because he was my hero that I didn't see his flaws. He had them and was willing to list them for you, if you earned his respect. I knew him to be stubborn (with a capital "S"), proud (I can do it!), narrow-minded (right is right!), impatient (what's the problem?), racist (isn't God a WASP?), and insensitive (after all, right is right). But, he was kind, helpful, dependable, fair, responsible, strong, persistent, consistent, caring, and humble. His humility was knowing exactly who he was and accepting both the limitations and the glory of what God had given him. That is the foundation for my own definition of humility.

Bill always spoke of God in terms that left no doubt about who was ultimately in charge. That was, in large part, the substance of the serenity he found in this life and the next. Bill knew that, although he might or might not be answerable to someone in this life, he would inevitably be answerable to God in the next, and he took that seriously.

My friend Bill was a patriot. He was an American patriot both in an era when there was glory in that statement and in times when there was social tarnish in the epithet. John Wayne never helped me love my country more that Bill did, over our endless campfire talks, Bill taught me about the responsibility and honor of standing up for your flag, your country and your fellow citizens. Bill marched to the drumbeat of Valley Forge and was so proud to be an American. After a weekend with Bill, I was ready to sign up and fight for my country. As proud of being an American as he was, that is how proud I am to have known him. He honored us; I honor him.

I don't claim to know him anywhere near as well as his wife, his, son, or grandchildren. They certainly knew aspects of him that I will never know. But, I think I was privileged to share a part of him that could only have happened to the right person in the right place at the right time (see-right IS right!). My view of Bill isn't correct or incorrect – it's just my view. I wouldn't trade it for anything in the world, because it's precious to me – no, it's part of me.

So, where is my friend Bill? He's right where he is supposed to be and deserves to be. He's with "the Man upstairs." With a little luck, he's sitting around a campfire with a few other campers. I suspect they're congratulating each other on finally being able to prove what they knew all along – that what's right is really right. Bill, if you are listening, I want you to know that you "done good' with your friend Peter. I don't need a hero anymore, but I'd appreciate it if you'd save a place around that campfire for me. I'll be home soon and it will be so, so good to see your smiling face again. I miss you, my friend…I really do!

᠑᠑᠑

Stu Canham was my best friend during my hazy days of adolescence. In 1978 he was a management level employee of the Singer Corporation and had a magnificent house on the Front Range with a view of Pike's Peak. We spent many evenings drinking beer on his deck watching the famous Colorado sunsets that John Denver referred to as," fire in the sky." Stu died February 5, 1999 of stomach cancer. In October 1998 when he knew he was failing, Stu came back to NY for a visit. I knew it was to say goodbye. I drove him to Bay Ridge in Brooklyn where we both lived as teenagers. He wanted to see the apartment house he grew up in. I snapped a photo of him standing in front of its entrance.

Stu on Eighth Ave, Brooklyn

We both tried to decipher the language spoken by the three men working on a car in front of the building. Eighth Avenue between 48th and 49th Street always bore a multi-ethnic identity. Back in the 1950's it was made up of Irish, Norwegian, German, and Italian. Now there was a distinct

Chinese and Hispanic flavor. The three men working on the car fit none of these groups. Their origin is still a mystery to me.

Stu and I went to the local bar in which many of us from that neighborhood came of age. We began our legal drinking at the age of eighteen. Lento's is on the corner of Eighth Avenue and 54th Street owned by brothers Joe and Frank was still there. Stu, who had far more experience in barroom environments than I, immediately was entrenched in conversation. In a matter of minutes, he found out where people that had been absent from our lives for forty years were.

We were soon across the street in another bar. This one was without patrons at the time. We were there to see the bartender, Tom Lundy. As a child, Stu was quite close to the Lundy family. Tom, I remembered as being part of the softball team called the Flynn Celtics. We played against them. Tom was the younger of his two great athlete brothers, Bobby and Franny. I played for the Vikings. We never came close to beating them.

I then drove Stu to Dyker Park to look for Pete Simonetti. Like us, he was another Pershing Junior High School graduate from the early 1950's. We found Pete, playing cards outdoors, with a group of other retired guys our age. While we were there, a pizza delivery appeared which included more than pizza. There was a distinct sausage and pepper aroma coming from the generous sized Italian hero sandwiches.

I couldn't bring myself to admit it, but Stu knew he was dying and was saying goodbye. And did it with dignity. I miss Stu too.

I remember the correspondence we had before his death.

I received a letter from Stu in April 1998. I was devastated because he announced the state of his poor health. I sent him the following reply:

Dated April 17, 1998

Dear Stu

It took me one entire day to digest the meaning or your letter. It took me another day to plan this response to you. I realize you are a very important part of my life. You helped shape my character. I am very moved by the news of your condition. In my 59 years of a diverse life, I haven't crossed paths with a tougher individual than you. Not only is your toughness paramount in my mind, but so is your ability to fight. You taught me to fight when I was a fourteen-year-old kid who was a reject from the mean streets of a Brooklyn adolescent culture. I felt unaccepted in that unique society because of my Jewish identity. An identity I did not want. I was rejected by the Jewish kids east of Ninth Avenue because they knew I wasn't a full Jew. Similarly, I was rejected by the melting pot of Italian, Irish, and German kids on the West side of Ninth Avenue. My last name was Finkelstein.

Not until I met up with you did I feel accepted for who I was. It was you who taught me to confront the demons of adolescence. It was you who back then, taught me to be a street fighter. Side by side, we fought well together in those many Eighth Avenue and Sunset Park fights we endured.

Remember Sean Conner? He was the kid who was 6'3' when the rest of us kids were 5'5. He couldn't speak; he just grunted and communicated in single word sentences. In our younger years he kept us free from the bullying of the 50th Street Boys. Then there was Morris the Masturbator. Remember when he told us that he used his mother's vacuum cleaner to masturbate? We all fell down from laughing so hard. Then there was the time when we told the older boys that Anthony practiced bestiality with Ginger, the always pregnant stray dog in our neighborhood. Remember how concerned the older guys were. They said that Ginger was all diseased and we should never do that because it was a sin.

Those were fun days Stu.

Again, it is you who is teaching me to confront those demons. This time they are demons of adulthood. Like we were when we were teenagers, we will fight together. I want to help. The last time I prayed hard for anything was 50 years ago. I prayed for the Yankees to beat the Brooklyn Dodgers in the 1947 World Series. My prayers were answered then. Tuesday night I prayed again, I prayed for the remission I know you can achieve. You will have many more years of life, of fishing, of camping, of high altitude highs, of family gatherings, of pure enjoyment. I know you can do it. I've seen you fight. I've seen your argument ending, one-punch knock outs. Like the time you hit Pete McNamara, remember that punch? His eye was black before he hit the ground. You'll do it again. You have to! People need you. Your kids need you. Hell, I need you. For example, when I called Alex at work to tell him of your letter, his voice took on a low thick sound I have never heard from him before. Shit man, he needs you too!

I spent yesterday doing some research. I also made some calls. I spoke to three cancer survivors. One person in particular, my cousin Joanie in Tampa: She had cancer throughout her body; among the organs affected were her lungs and liver. Sound familiar? She is going on her fourth year of remission. Her hair has grown back, she is healthy and happy.

Each of these people have one thing in common, they are fighters,they all wanted life and they still have it.

From the research I did I found there are several approaches you can take. In addition to the conventional chemo treatment, there are holistic strategies. These work! Diet changes, including vitamin doses to enhance your immune system and meditation techniques. Dr. Rosemary Pilkington, also a cousin of mine and an atheist revealed that prayer, even from people many miles away, and daily meditation works. She divulges that something, an energy, exists that has put cancer into remission in many patients.

As I see it, a combination of diet, vitamins and meditation along with conventional medical treatment is the way to go.

Meditation trains your mind to concentrate on one non threatening thing at a time. You do it for about 20 minutes a day. Transcendental Meditation was made popular by the Beatles in the 60's. This is a technique where a person sits in a quiet spot and continually repeats a mantra. The mantra could be the words, Hare Krishna, Kyre Elision, Peace on Earth or even a nonsensical rhyme like, Twiddle Dum, Twiddle Dee. What each of these mantras has in common is that they isolate the mind on one simple thought. When said out loud, some experts say the resonation (buzz) enhances the relaxation effect.

One boy I read about survived a growing inoperable brain tumor, was taught to imagine a group of tiny workmen *in painters coveralls each with a large push broom scrubbing away his tumor. The boy did this daily meditation and has gone down in medical history because of what was an diagnosed as an inoperable terminal condition, became non-existent.*

I will come to see you this June, around the second. I can't get away before then.

I also found, at the library yesterday, that a healthy diet, embellished with a daily dose of vitamins is also necessary to develop a healthy immune system. I suppose you stopped your alcohol intake. I'm sure your doctors told you that alcohol promotes cancer while at the same time suppresses the immune system.

Keep me informed of your location. It seems that Patrick has really come through for you. You must be very proud of him. Give my regards to Patrick, Sean, Tim and Terri and the rest of your family.

I am glad you wrote. Sometimes it takes a crisis to let a person know what is really important in life. That was a devastating letter you sent but at the same time you put beauty into it. I'm glad you put the addresses of your kids in there. It's good to have contact. As you well know our kids spent many summers together. We will do it again. I will stay in touch.

Sincerely,
Alex

Stu's response came as follows:

Dated June 29, 1998;

Dear friends and relatives:

Here is the medical update on my progress to date.

First, I wish to thank each and every one of you for the concern, empathy and assistance you have given me in my time of need.

Your cards, flowers gifts, phone calls and physical presence have been at times, overwhelming.

There is a force in this world and you are it. God is the ultimate force, but he gave it to us. He has given us power. There is the power of concentration, and then there is the concentration of power. You don't know how powerful you are and what you all have meant to me. With your continued help, I will overcome my illness, keep it up. I feel that power every day and I need it.

Well, it's been three months since my surgery In that time, Brother Don and Maryanne have visited me in the hospital. I wish there was more time to socialize, but illness on both sides prevented it. It was a short but great visit. I was in the hospital over St. Patrick's Day and the kids went all out to make it festive. Flowers, shamrocks, green hats and all. It was as good as it could be under the circumstances.

Daughter Terri and son Tim came out to visit during my recovery and we had the opportunity to visit the Celtic festival in Kiowa, CO.

We had the whole family together for a day of games and festival, marching bands, step dancers pipes, etc. It was another great day topped off by the biggest lasagna feast in many a year.

My good friend, Al Flint from Brooklyn also stopped by on his visit to Colorado and we had a fine day of fishing in Cherry Creek Reservoir and visiting.

Once again, THANK YOU for everything.

In these three months, I have had my six sessions of chemotherapy. I do not know the results yet, but when I know, you will know. The chemo is given at a local hospital. I go once a week for about three hours. I am fed breakfast to forestall nausea. I am given a group of drugs designed to mitigate the effects of chemo, intravenously, for about an hour. I am them given the dose of cancer killer, then another hour of mitigation. My side effects to the chemo have so far been mild. Some slight nausea, diarrhea, and a slight skin problem. I have also experienced some thinning of the hair, but don't we all? All in all, it is not as bad as it could have been. The best thing of all is I have had little or no pain and this amazes the nursing staff. They can't believe I had a colostomy and still can be in high spirits. I also have gained twenty pounds, regained some of my muscle, have a healthy complexion and most people say I look very fit for a guy who has cancer and has been through what I have been through.

Now for the really good news. This past weekend I had my colostomy reversed! I had my intestines reattached and the dreaded ostomy bag is gone. Now I can squat and shit like a human being again. You will never know what a blow to your self image is unless you had to handle that vital but horrible experience. I get my stitches out next week, and at this time all functions appear to be normal. While in the hospital, they also inserted a "shunt" or "port" in my upper chest, (a plastic device or implant to facilitate future chemotherapy.) The constant use of needles and chemicals has been damaging to the veins of my hands and arms, and this is supposed to be better. I feel like a character from the X Files. That and the scars on my stomach that look like a railroad switch yard have given me one more life experience. Now I can say one more thing, "been there, done that."

Now, for some future plans. I intend to maintain the chemo treatment as needed. I opted for a very aggressive plan, and I advised the doctor that we are not talking about containment or control, we are talking about elimination!!!!

I have been doing weight training again and with my appetite back and the ability to eat well, my goal is 160 lbs with the proper distribution of weight.

I am currently on Colorado "old age pension," which in reality is a disability pension available to seniors. I get $530 a month put into a credit card format, Medicare, and $120 a month for food stamps. This is a big help, but of course unlivable, especially in the Colorado economy. I thank the generosity of my son and daughter in law, Patrick and Kris, for offering me a home.

They are planning to move to Brush, Colorado very soon and it is my intention to go with them, but it won't be permanent. I have applied for federal SSI, which is nothing more that the same program I am on now, but paid by the feds instead of Colorado. It also allows for the ability to work to some degree with no major loss of benefits. I have also applied for SSD, (social security disability) which will have a major impact on my income. I have been on disability for six months before I am even eligible for that, but I earned it and it I can get it, all the better. My six months will be up in September at which time I will be 61. Halfway to the one year 50/50 scenario. Then, for better or worse, it will only be one more year before I can take early retirement through regular Social Security. Tell me I won't make it to retirement.

During all this, it is my goal to visit Tim in Ocean City, Maryland sometime during late August or early September. I will see the local sights, then on to NY with Tim to visit relatives. I will get to stay a few days with Alex on Staten Island and visit the old haunts in Brooklyn. Plans are vague then. As always, Art, Angie and family are right on the way and it is only a short hop to Terri in Peoria.

So until next time, keep me in your thoughts, and may those thought be positive, positive for both you and me.

Love to you all,
Stu

With the Canhams the Arkansas River

I will surely miss Stu. He helped shape my character and personality. Stu taught me rules for street survival. He taught me to play cards like I never knew was possible. He showed me the technique for stacking a deck and how to cut the deck with one hand. He also showed me how to deal from the bottom of the deck without being caught. The key to this, he said, was to have the players distracted. Stu demonstrated how the back design of professional decks of cards is decorated with symbols that are in multiples of thirteen. By marking one of those designs it would indicate what the value of the card was on the other side. That is why casinos always change decks and open them from fresh boxes in front of the gamblers. In Sunset Park we always played with the same deck. It was the one Stu conveniently had in his back pocket. With practice we were able to give cryptic signals to each other. Many a victim in poker games in Sunset Park are still wondering why we always came out winners in those penny ante games.

Regarding fighting skills, Stu showed me the proper way to punch. "Keep a straight line between your elbow and knuckles," he would say. "That will do the most damage."

With Stu, 1989

Stu demonstrated the art of distraction. He said if the time comes and you know you are about to get jumped, distract your opponent and then try to pick a critical target, like the jaw or nose before you strike. He also showed how to grab your antagonist's belt buckle and pull it towards you while simultaneously bringing your knee up into his groin. As a fourteen-year-old, I was amazed as to how much street smarts my new found friend had.

In 1979, my daughter Debbie came with Alex and me. We stayed at the Canham's in their spacious Castle Rock home and continued the adventures we had begun the previous year. Stu took us to Deckers, and a campground on the Colorado River.

With Alex and Debbie, Colorado River Campsite

In 1991, Chuck and Arlene planned a trip to Europe. They asked if I would manage their ranch while they were gone. "Sure," I said, "I'd love that." That was a great summer. My daughters, Nancy and Betsy along with my son, flew out and we had a grand time at the ranch. Like me, my kids fell in love with Bill, the thoroughbred, former race horse.

Arlene's daughter-in-law Becky Donlan lived nearby and owned two horses. She told us the horses were in need of exercise and it would be a favor if Nancy and Betsy would ride them. Wow, that was great. We arranged to do an overnighter and haul the horses up to the Colorado Trail. Becky had a horse trailer and along with Becky's daughter Alicia, we had a memorable adventure. Becky's horses were Blackjack, a black Appaloosa and Shasta, a white Appaloosa and as horses go, were sweethearts. Betsy and Nancy wanted to take them home. "Daddy," Nancy said, "They are calm, gentle and so loving."

Betsy and Friends, Colorado Trail

The state of Colorado maintained the Colorado Trail for hikers and horse riders. Becky knew of a corral up on the trail that we used to hold the horses for the night while we curled up in our sleeping bags nearby. The air at that altitude was crisp, clear and cool that night. Its low humidity allowed the smoke from the campfire to have a special fragrance that cannot be duplicated. It's a memory we will hold for the rest of our lives.

Among the thrills we had at that high altitude was the roar of a mountain lion. He was probably letting us know we were trespassing in his territory. While riding on the trail, it was also noticeable the horses were quite in need of exercise because we were forced to spend a good part of the time walking them. One of them actually lay right down on the trail. During those exciting childhood Saturday matinees, we never saw that happen to Roy Rogers and Trigger.

Becky Donlan is a Colorado transplant from Texas. She is the epitome of a self-sufficient woman. She made the best barbeque brisket we ever had. In fact, I don't believe I ever had brisket prepared that way before. It was awesome and I will never forget it.

Very proud of her part Native American heritage, Becky is president of the Native American Research and Preservation Corporation. She is passionately involved with locating, documenting, researching and preserving prehistoric and historic Native American sites. She recently worked with the Smithsonian Institution in discovering ancient rock art and stone circles. Becky also works with the USDA Forest Service, the Bureau of Land Management, the Colorado State Land Office and the National Park Service.

Becky on the Colorado Trail

Becky is also involved with educating the public. She teaches never to pick up or take any artifacts. "Where an object is, is as important as *what* it is." Instead, she instructs: take photographs or draw sketches. We learn by what is left behind, but the story is destroyed when artifacts are taken or moved. She also points out, that buying artifacts only encourages looting of these important historical sites.

The world was made a better place when Becky was born.

On a memorable day I drove Nancy, Betsy and Alex to Aspen, 50 miles to the northwest as the crow flies. We could not drive as straight as a crow, so the trip took most of the day. We drove north from Salida toward Leadville on Route 24. Turning left at Balltown, we steered on to Independence Pass Road. This took us past Mount Elbert,

14,433 high. It is typically beautiful mountain country. As we began our incline we passed Twin Lakes Reservoir. Chuck would often say of this country, "It's beautiful because it's so close to heaven."

Betsy and Nancy, Picking Flowers

When we arrived in Aspen, it was as though we were planted in another universe. From the agricultural ranch life we knew for the last few weeks, we were immersed in a different culture. Mosaic and brick sidewalks and flower-laden plazas surrounded us. A well tanned George Hamilton walked passed us on several occasions and always greeted us with a warm smile. I wasn't sure if his eyes were on Nancy or Betsy. It was then suggested his smile was directed at Alex. I'm sure he was motivated by the female attraction of my daughters.

After taking in the clean beauty of that resort town,

Nancy made her now famous comment, "Salida, Shmilida, I love Aspen!"

Nancy Loving Aspen

♪♪♪

As the stories of our adventures circulated on Staten Island, I was able to get friends to meet me in The Rockies. One memorable occasion was in the summer of 1983 when Gerry Rahelich, a fellow teacher at Susan E. Wagner High School, met us in the Grand Teton National Park. I had given him an approximate date that I would be in Jenny Lake. Now, you have to understand this was in 1983 before the days of cell phone or wireless devices. I was pleasantly surprised one evening when I spotted him driving through the narrow dirt road of the Jenny Lake Campground.

The following year I was met in the same campground

Alex, Gerry Rahelich, Gerry Jr.

by fellow Staten Islanders Zeke Quin and his friend Greg DeForest. Zeke and his buddy followed us from Wyoming to Stu's house in Castle Rock, Colorado. We spent a week there to Stu's elation. Regarding alcohol intake, Zeke was able to keep up with Stu, a fellow Irishman, much better than I ever could. Those guys happily drank till the sun rose while playing Irish music. I remember getting up for my morning run at dawn as they were just getting ready for sleep.

♪♪♪

It was 1999 as I left the ranch pulling a trailer with my Harley attached. The sky in the East bore a rosy tint as I left Salida before dawn. There was a light rain falling as I headed north on Colorado State Highway 285. After 18 miles, the road swung to the east and drew me closer to the brilliance of the beautiful sky. I felt a lump in my throat. I was familiar with that sad feeling. For two decades when the elements force me, like a homing pigeon, to return to my home on Staten Island, the sadness was always there. I already missed the sounds of the Arkansas

River and the residents of The Ute Valley Ranch. Chuck's creation still is there. The log house was a magnet to Flicka the Blue Heeler, a herding dog who likes to keep things in place. That included things like the many picket pins, a small meerkat style rodent. He watched over two orange tabby cats who miraculously survived from last year. Cats that are not careful fall prey to the great horned owls and coyotes who own the night. Occasionally Flicka will try to chase the numerous birds that Arlene feeds through her feeding stations. Among these feathered beauties are pine siskins, pinion jays, numerous broad tailed humming birds and the regal Lewis Woodpecker. Arlene, a Martha Stewart/Abigal VanBuren/Heloise type, was Chuck's wife. She recently married Ernest Pennington, Chuck's friend, a widower who owns the neighboring ranch. They are two wonderful people.

Flicka, the Blue Heeler

Saying goodbye to horses for me is like the scene from *The Yearling*, a 1940's movie with Gregory Peck who tells his son he must kill his pet deer. It is a real tearjerker. Horses do something to me that bring me back to my Saturday matinee hero, Roy Rogers and the connection he had with his horse Trigger. Every morning at the ranch, as I would walk down to the river's edge, the three horses would vie for the position to be closest to me. It sort of gave me the feeling of being appreciated just for my presence. It was always the same routine and I got to like it. In past years the horses were looking to be fed, but this year due to the excess of rain they had all the sweet green grass they could eat. They just wanted me, man. How could you not miss a daily greeting like that?

Nancy with Bill

As I approached I-25, my thoughts wandered to Stu Canham and his family. They lived in Castle Rock to the South. My trip would not take me there this year.

I steered toward the Northeast. I left I-70 and guided my Lincoln on to I-76 that would take me to Nebraska. Denver was behind me and traffic would be much lighter now. I would now drive for miles without seeing any north-bound traffic. I left the rocky mountain section of Colorado and was now entering the high plains. As I did so, the Denver classic rock radio stations would grow weaker and my CD would be switched on and Willie Nelson would again fill the Lincoln with his relaxing sounds. While the Ute Indians lived in the South Park area, the Comanche, Kiowa, and the Cheyenne were the inhabitants of these plains that were loaded with bison. Seventy million years or so ago this was a sea. Chuck gave me a fossilized seashell he found on his ranch, and emphasized that his high altitude rocky mountain ranch was once under water.

As I continued my eastward journey, I was overwhelmed with a melancholy feeling. I had felt this way before, like, every time I began my trip home. I knew that after the first twelve hours of driving I would begin to be inundated with thoughts of my Staten Island home. I knew my Rottweiler Ava would be waiting. She was an affectionate 85 pound bundle of muscle and energy. I knew from previous trips to Florida, Germany and Colorado that an enormous welcoming ritual was awaiting me. She would be a bit flabbier and her coat a few shades duller. She would spend her days awaiting my return with her nose breathing the air coming from under the closed door to my bedroom. She would be depressed. She missed me and her morning and evening walks. We take walks of at least 30 minutes duration because she refuses to return sooner. She gets to go wherever her powerful heart desires. Ava seems intent upon leaving her scent at numerous strategic locations. In addition, she has certain places in which she would gouge small ravines with her paws. I have come to the conclusion that she is marking territory and communicating with another dog that lives nearby. This is probably a primitive instinct left over from the days when her ancient canine ancestors roamed in packs and terrorized all other four-legged inhabitants. Now she only terrorizes the residents of New Dorp that cross her path. Ava has to miss me, because when else can she follow her primal desire to mark territory? Her welcoming ceremony is something I am anticipating. I never had a wife to lather me with a wet tongue like that when I return home from a trip. Or lay down at my feet in an ecstasy brought on by just my presence. Although, come to think of it, I never had a wife I walked with for a half hour or more, twice a day or spent so much time with. Maybe that's the answer to a happy marriage?

ᴊᴊᴊ

About this time I reached I-80 East I was 125 miles from the Wyoming border. I was in Nebraska now and approaching Ogallala. This old cowboy town is located at the end of the Chisolm Trail. Larry McMurtry wrote of it in his bestselling book, *Lonesome Dove*.

We first stopped here in 1973. It was my first trip to the West. Along with Irene and our five kids, our 1969 Ford Country Squire station wagon carried us in style. I remember it was the end of our fourth day of traveling after leaving Staten Island and the Holiday Inn in Ogallala was a welcome sight. The motel backed up to the Platte River. It was July and the river was dry. I couldn't believe it. I had never seen a dry river before. The distance to the other bank was about 200 yards and it was dusty. It was my first time away from the East Coast and had no experience with an arid climate. The ground was brown and the vegetation was yellow. Nothing was green except the cottonwood trees. I later learned that cottonwoods can adapt to long periods of dryness. The sky was the bluest I had ever seen and the air was fresh and clear with a fragrance new to me. I absolutely loved it.

The kids' expended energy built up after so many hours in the car with much needed playtime in the pool. We got a bit of sunburn and felt the ultra dry air chill our skin as it quickly evaporated the water on our skin when we got out of the water. I am sure there are many science teachers in the humid East that would love to teach a lesson on evaporation here with their classes.

That time in 1973 is among my fondest of memories. Ogallala would afford me no respite from the driving now though. I only stop here on the way west. I guess I try to relive that happy time with Irene and the kids. As I passed Ogallala at the legal speed limit of 70 mph, I thought of the way we spent that evening twenty-six years ago. We had dinner in the Crystal Palace, a restaurant with stage and saloon located in an old west restoration area. I drank red beer and ate mountain oysters. That is, beer mixed with tomato juice and fried breaded bull testicles dipped in hot sauce. I remember immediately identifying with cowboy life and wanting to buy a ten gallon hat. Man that was such a happy time. The kids were called up on stage and were made part of the show. The actors where dressed in period clothing as cowboys and dance hall girls. In one of the scenes the kids we part of, they sat in a stage prop wagon as the players sang *Clementine*. At the end of the show each of my kids were sworn in as deputy sheriffs and given shiny tin badges.

It was a great evening. I will always remember that

night as one of my proudest moments with my family.

After the show, as we were leaving, an elderly couple approached us. They were so very impressed with the good behavior of our kids they invited us to stay on their ranch. They said their children were grown and relocated in a big city somewhere. They loved our kids and mentioned how well-mannered they were. They commented on the way they conducted themselves in the restaurant and on stage. They said they would be honored if we stayed with them. I remember thanking them profusely but explaining we were to meet my Marine Corps buddy, Roy Howard at the Pepper Pod the next day. Roy's folks owned a restaurant in Hudson, Colorado that raised buffalos to be served as steaks. I'm sorry I never got the address of that Nebraska couple to send a letter thanking them for their offer.

I had 300 more miles in Nebraska, about six hours of driving. I would be leaving the west and entering the Great Plains, lots of long, large, great, plains. When I got to the next state, Iowa, I knew the humidity would be back. I was ready for it. I was going home.

ﺩﺩﺩ

My parents came to Salida in 1992. I picked them up at Stapleton Airport in Denver. We then drove through South Park on our way to Chuck's ranch. Dad got along well with Chuck. They were both retired NY City Firefighters, were about the same age and enjoyed taking pleasure in swapping names of coworkers they knew.

Dad kept commenting on the agricultural lifestyle that was so evident. As far as the eye could see was open range. Once, during a trail drive that crossed the highway, we

Arlene Jensen Milking Her Goats

had to wait for the steers to be moved along by the cow-boys on horseback. The traffic pattern did not suffer much because there was only one other car that came along during the 10 minute wait. Dad said he couldn't imagine this happening in NY. He indicated that the drivers on the Brooklyn-Queens Expressway would never stand for it. I am sure there would be a cacophony of horns, obscene hand gestures and possibly a few gunshots.

My mother was pleasantly surprised by the visit we made to Grimo's Italian Restaurant in Poncha Springs. She said the food was good. There is no better endorsement than one from my mother for an Italian restaurant whether it is from New York or from Italy. She was born in the Little Italy section of New York of Sicilian parents. She then spent most of her life perfecting the various aspects of Italian cooking. She practiced her art every Sunday for her only child and five grandchildren.

Becky's Horse Shasta

CHAPTER **2**

Starmiss

I am well past Ogallala now, heading east and approaching Grand Island, Nebraska. The Eagles CD had finished and I began to search for an FM rock music station. As I approached Route 2, which goes northwest towards Broken Bow, I thought of 1980. That was the year Alex and I took that route to Grand Tetons National Park. Thoughts of an unforgettable night were brought to the vanguard of my memory.

I called her Starmiss. I really don't remember her name, I don't know if she even told us. She was tall about 5'9", had big brown eyes, slim, like a fashion model, and exciting. She exuded a weird, though non-threatening aura, and was a pleasure to be with. She was traveling light with just a backpack and attached sleeping bag. She was hitchhiking at the north end of Broken Bow, at a gas station where we had stopped to replenish the ice in our Coleman chest. I was driving my 1978 Chevy conversion van that Alex named Darth Vader. It was completely black with a ladder and continental wheel mounted in the back. The interior was bright red. On the highway this streaking black box appeared like a huge jewel.

Darth Vader, 1978 Chevy Van

Starmiss was on her way to San Francisco where a waitress job was waiting for her. She wanted to earn enough money to study to become an actress. I told her we were going to the Tetons and she asked if we would mind some company.

༄༄༄

I once vowed to never pick up hitchhikers again since I stopped for a wet dude I had pitied. There was a tropical downpour that afternoon. You know the hotsummer afternoon kind that is always accompanied by thunder. I was driving in Union, NJ while on my way to take a summer course at Kean College. As he climbed into my 1968 VW Bug, I asked that he drop his lit cigarette outside. He began to argue that he just lit it up and kept it as he sat in my car. I almost committed a capital offense that rainy afternoon. I became so infuriated because I thought I was doing a favor for someone who was in dire need of one. On that damp, rainy, sinus irritating day, an asshole would get in my car and not want to put his cigarette out. Fortunately, luck was with him because he was able to break free from my grasp and escape into the rain.

Starmiss bore no such negative karma. She was a purely lovable person. She was, I believe, the original, Holly Golightly, the character Audrey Hepburn played in *Breakfast at Tiffanies*. Starmiss loved nature, peanut butter sandwiches, and Leonard Skynard. She was a totally relaxed individual. Ulcers would never form in her digestive tract. We drove on to Thermopolis, WY, where we spent the night in a Holiday Inn. We stood before one of the multicolored, steaming, mineral laden, water eruptions from the ground. That is what Thermopolis is known for. She stood before it eyes closed and in deep meditation. When I asked what she was doing, she whispered, "I am communing with spirits gathered before me." I immediately began to question my wisdom of picking up a stranger and decided I would sleep lightly that night.

My fears were unfounded and the next morning we drove on to the Tetons. We got set up in a campsite at Jenny Lake Campground in the Grand Tetons National Park. The national park is located about ten miles north of Jackson WY. The Jenny Lake campground is rather small and only allows tent camping. The view is like nothing I have ever seen. In the early morning Jenny Lake was like a mirrored sea. The only ripples would be from a duck or a far off swimming beaver.

Vehicle-mounted or pulled trailers, along with their noisy air conditioners, generators and music that disrupts nature, were, thankfully, not allowed. Other campgrounds far away from this pristine, primeval location do permit trailers and huge motor homes with their offending noise and light pollution to contaminate nature. This Jenny Lake campground is quiet and dark at night and clearly simulates the natural surroundings. We set up our small tent and took a hike. We followed a trail in a northerly direction to String Lake. The three-mile trail which followed the clear water along its edge was primordial. We walked under a canopy of thick dark green pine boughs which hung out over the water like triumphant banners. The silence of the 8,000-foot high lake was in far contrast to what we were used to on Staten Island. We could see a beaver swimming parallel to us as we walked north. I think the beautiful creature was as curious about us as we were of him. When the beaver slapped his tail on the glasslike surface it cracked like a lion tamer's whip. Was he attracting our attention? Starmiss said he was a reincarnated Indian welcoming us to his land.

The Grand Tetons were named by French trappers that frequented the area in the early half or the nineteenth century. It is said that when they first sighted the three magnificent 14,000-foot high cones, they were overcome with emotion. They were later named the Grand, Middle and South Teton. These trappers, who were away from the sight of a woman's body for many months, were reminded of female breasts. They must have been away a long, long time.

Geologists tell us this impressive vista was formed by enormous physical activity deep under the earth's surface many millions of years ago. As underground plates ground themselves together one massive fault block was forced upward and the other downward. The upper mass, on the western side rose thousands of feet over the valley floor to create the Tetons. The beauty and dramatic appearance we enjoy today is because of the lack of foothills to the east of these enormous peaks. The Front Range in Colorado does have foothills thereby preventing the viewer from seeing such an immediate six thousand foot rise. The peak of Mount Moran, one of the impressive Tetons, possesses the same geological makeup, stones, gems and minerals, as that of the valley floor more than 25,000 feet beneath the surface. Geologists offer this as evidence of the enormous disruption of real estate so many eons ago.

There was an open sunny spot where the water of String Lake was shallow and warmed by the high altitude summer sun. Starmiss asked if I minded if she took a dip. I thought it was a great idea and inquired if she brought a bathing suit along. She smiled and indicated she didn't need one. I soon realized there were a lot of things she didn't need. The plastic surgeons that make their living from women seeking perfection via a medical sculpture's skill would starve if all women had a body like hers. Once she removed her baggy painter's pants and loose sweatshirt her concealed cache became exposed. If those French trappers saw her they would die of shock. I began to feel a funny rumble deep in my insides. The whiteness of her smooth skin made it apparent she did not spend much time in the sun. Her skin was as smooth as cream. I followed her as she immersed herself in the clear water. The water was warm near the shore, but as we swam further out and the sandy bottom fell away it soon became an arctic bath. Indeed, it was polar-like! We were swimming in water that was melting into the lake from the Mount St. John Glacier directly above us.

Cold Glacial Water

It was embarrassingly cold and my manhood was reduced to a mere stub which became pitifully noticeable as we exited the water. At that point I was sorry I did not wear a bathing suit and realized that women were luckier in this respect. There is no shrinkage upon their points of pride from cold water for them; it only makes them look more alluring.

Back at the campsite Starmiss impressed Alex with a lesson in fire starting. She built a 'Lincoln Log' structure using pencil sized twigs. The sticks formed a square that became narrower as it rose to its height of about fourteen inches. The center was filled with dry leaves and grass. When it was ignited at the bottom there was a blaze in almost no time at all. Larger sticks and branches were then added. I cut logs with the bowsaw I kept in the van. There was an adequate wood supply from the many downed trees in the adjacent forest that would feed our campfire well into the night.

Starmiss explained that this was the method the Indians used. She went on to tell us that Blackfeet, Crow, Gros Ventre, and Shoshone would spend their summers in this valley on the eastern side of the mountain range. These Native Americans considered this neutral territory and shared its resources. I found it interesting that these tribes possessed their own territory they would have gone to war over if encroached on. Interestingly though in this place of natural beauty they shared the land. Early man entered Jackson Hole, as this area is called, about 12,000 years ago. He has remained ever since.

From the time we got back to the camp, I couldn't wait to impress my new found Holly Golightly friend with my culinary expertise. I had a Coleman gasoline stove with which I boiled water to cook the spaghetti. I made a simple oglia oilio sauce. That is, garlic and olive oil. The meal was followed by espresso spiked with anisette. This was so incongruent because we were at an altitude of 8,500 feet. We camped across from crystal clear, Jenny Lake which was bordered by Mount Moran, Mount Owen and Mount St. John. Their peaks rose to fourteen thousand on the west shore. Our campsite was on the east shore thereby giving us an impressive sunset which reflected its majestic glow on the lake's waters. The oglia oilio pasta was popular on far-off Elizabeth Street, in the Little Italy section of New York City, where I was born. It made an impression on Starmiss. I was proud of myself. I had hopes of getting lucky that night.

Alex went to sleep in the van about ten o'clock. Starmiss and I lay out by the campfire on sleeping bags and watched the stars come into view. There was no moon and the stars just kept on emerging. This was the beginning of a show the likes of which I had never before seen. The clarity of these Teton stars was the most awesome I ever witnessed. Starmiss told me how special stars were to her. She asked if I knew their names. From my US Marine Corps Basic School map reading course, I showed her Polaris, Orion's belt and the two Dippers. She then showed me Lydia, which she said was a childhood special friend who died before she was a teenager. Then she showed me Justin and Mark and Mary Ellen, She had them named for all special people. She even showed me her Mother and Father. I thought, "Wow, she is really far out." She then asked me if I wanted a special treat. I had an idea of what was coming, I had been hoping for more than a day now and was delighted. Instead of what I expected, she reached into her backpack and brought out what looked like a dried apricot. She ate a piece and gave me the rest. I asked what it was and she said it was a magic mushroom. Well, not since I read *Alice in Wonderland* did I hear of mushrooms altering one's state. I was uninformed as to the properties of fungi. That was soon to change.

I really am not sure how much time passed. It may have been about fifteen minutes when Starmiss' voice became softer and smoother. Was the mushroom causing this transformation? I was lying on my back staring at the stars when I noticed a strangeness occurring in the universe. First there was a shooting star that flashed across our front. Then there was another, and then another, it seemed as though the shooting stars rapidly became brighter and more abundant. As the seconds passed the sky became darker and the stars more intense, then it seemed the shooting stars began to change direction. I was experiencing a pyrotechnics demonstration better than the fourth of July. Starmiss was lying across my chest now and we were nude.

Remarkably, I don't remember undressing. How did this happen? It was like a movie being edited from one scene to another where the continuity was disrupted. She began kissing my cheek and her long straight brown hair slid across my eyes. I became conscious of many strange feelings. While I wanted to continue to observe the star show, I was also motivated to avert my attention to this incredibly sensual creature. She was now softly sliding her lips across my stomach. I was relieved she moved away from my face because I wanted to continue to view the heavens. I had been anticipating her warmth for more than a day. Now the time was here and I was more interested in the stars. Was I going crazy? Where were my priorities? Do I follow my instincts and make wild love to Starmiss, or do I succumb to the attraction in the sky above?

My senses quickly returned. The stars would have to wait. They would be there later. The stars will always be there. Now was the time for the primitive pleasure of nature to continue. We rolled around on, out of, and off the sleeping bags. We soon lay on the forest floor. It seemed like we had all our body parts touching at the same time. The feelings and sensations brought on by *Wonderland* mushrooms were beyond belief. Was it this woman with a magical charm? Was it the stars? Maybe it was the altitude? I didn't care, it didn't matter. I just followed my instincts. There was the contrast of the warmth of our bodies touching and the chill of the Wyoming mountain air touching our exposed skin. The aroma of espresso, garlic, olive oil, and campfire all combined like the melding of the delicious flavors of a tortellini. This was an experience I would never forget. No, not ever!

Before we parted, Starmiss showed me a collection of what she called "toilet wisdom." She had copied graffiti she found in ladies' rest rooms in her travels hitchhiking across the country. I was so moved by these philosophical words, I asked if I could copy it. She was flattered that her hobby so interested me. They are as follows:

Friends don't let friends take home ugly men.
A Filling Station, Wilmington, DE

Remember, it's not "How high are you?" its "Hi, how are you?"
Rest stop off the Ohio Turnpike, Toledo, Ohio

Make love, not war. Hell, do both, get married!
A Filling Station, Bozeman, Montana

A Woman's Rule of Thumb: If it has tires or testicles, you're going to have trouble with it.
A Filling Station, Amarillo, Texas

Beauty is only a light switch away.
Filling Station, Indiana Turnpike, IN

Fighting for peace is like screwing for virginity.
Rest Stop, Pennsylvania Turnpike, State College, PA

After seeing the humor and intellect that went into these statements, I too got the idea to collect graffiti statements from the numerous men's room visits made on my trips. I always thought of Starmiss as I wrote down the following pieces of prose:

Oklahoma is made up of Texans on their way to Colorado but could not find their way.
Public toilet at the Jenny Lake Campground, Grand Teton National Park, Wyoming.

No matter how good she looks, some other guy is tired of putting up with her crap.
Rest Stop, Interstate 80 Grand Island, Nebraska

No wonder you always go home alone.
Written on a mirror in front of the urinal. Rest Stop, Cheyenne, WY

It's hard to make a comeback when you haven't been anywhere.
Rest Stop, Interstate 80, Council Bluffs, Iowa

Don't trust anything that bleeds for five days and doesn't die.
Rest Stop, Interstate 80, Grand Island, Nebraska

What are you writing on the wall for? The joke is in your hands.
Rest Stop, Ft Collins, Colorado

Please don't throw your cigarette butts in the urinal. It makes them soggy and hard to light. The Janitor.
Filling Station, Longmont, Colorado

He who writes upon these walls,
Rolls his shit in little balls.
He who reads these words of wit,
Eats these little balls of shit!
Restaurant, Boulder, Colorado

After collecting these pieces of scripture, I wondered as to what kind of person it is that is motivated to spend their time doing this?

I don't remember saying goodbye to Starmiss and I do not remember missing her. First there was life without her, then she was there, and then she was gone. Our vacation went on, our lives continued. She went off to continue her life. I sometimes wonder about her. I wonder about where she is. Did she ever get the waitress job in San Francisco? Did she go on to an acting career? Sometimes when I see a shooting star on a moonless starlit night I think about that wonderful creature. I hope she is happy wherever she is.

CHAPTER **3**

Awake at the Wheel

I am alone again on the highway with my thoughts. I am still driving east toward the Nebraska-Iowa border. My new 1999 Silver Lincoln streaked out of my fantasy thoughts and back to the reality of getting in another eight or so hours of driving. This location on Interstate 80 was within the range of the FM stations of Lincoln and Omaha. I am thinking of home and listening to Billy Joel sing *Uptown Girl*.

Two decades ago these cities were separated by vast expanses of plains. They were now growing together like the megalopolises of the east. The highway, byways, overpasses, and traffic that abounds on I-80 in the Omaha area is reminiscent of any eastern major city. My thoughts shifted to an article I read recently about Sandhill Cranes. These huge birds stop in Nebraska during their migration and are having their feeding areas here being built upon. A good part of these cranes's diet is made up of rodents. If the crane population were to decline, the rodent population would rise, undoubtedly causing health problems.

During the middle ages the bubonic plague, the Black Death, killed off a major part of the population of Europe. A strain of this horrible disease has recently been found in the four corners region of the southwest. This is the area where the boundary lines of four states, Colorado, New Mexico, Arizona, and Utah come together at a single point. Habitat deprivation of our wild friends is a major problem throughout the world and is a major concern of naturalists. I know Starmiss would be worried; she felt that anything that created an imbalance of nature was wrong.

Cruising along at 70 MPH, I began to beat my thumbs on the steering wheel in time with Elton John's *Bennie and the Jets*. Some people play air guitar, I play dashboard drums. By shifting my thumbs as they strike the steering wheel's rim to the wheel's center, to the top of the shift lever, and to the dashboard, I can simulate the actions of Ringo Starr. When I get taken with this fantasy of being a drummer I become transformed to another plane, one with fun, friends, and happiness. By the time the song is finished I have traveled a pleasant five miles and have been transformed into a pleasant mood. This action gives me a needed break from the boredom of driving two thousand miles on this highway. It also gives me energy that will carry me many more miles eastward. Sometimes I play my harmonica to back up Willie Nelson. It too, is a great mood enhancer.

In the summer of 1980, I was waiting for Stu in a shopping area outside the Singer Sewing Center he owned in Castle Rock. Alex was inside helping his kids with some chore, and I was sitting in my van with the door open and my feet up on the dashboard. I was listening to KMJD 92 FM, a country music radio station. I was playing my Hohner along with the lively music. When the country song ended, Peggy Malone, the female disc jockey and country music star, began to describe over the air an interesting sight she was witnessing. It was of a guy sitting in his van with his feet up on the dashboard who was playing the harmonica. I must have sat up quickly and looked around because she then announced to her audience that I was listening to the station. Over the air, she then invited me to come in the studio to play. I couldn't believe it. I was completely bewildered. I had no idea where she or the studio were located and was astounded. I guess I looked like the people who are pranked on Candid Camera. She sent the station manager out to invite me in. After some persuading I accepted. I was interviewed and described myself as a NY City high school physical education teacher. I went on to say that

Country Singer Peggy Malone

with my son and van I travel to the Rocky Mountains every summer looking for adventure. She then asked me to play the harmonica while she spun *Orange Blossom Special* to her Denver audience. I did and will remember the moment far longer than she, I am sure.

♪♪♪♪

During my early years of driving this route the method of choice for maintaining alertness was Taylor's Pride chewing tobacco. It was potent stuff. Because I was unused to tobacco, I only needed about a five minute fix before I spit it all out. The energizing blast would last for about an hour.

When I got home that year I was invited to a barbecue at the Staten Island home of my friends Larry and Pat Ronaldson on Sharotts Road. In those days their house had woods around them that seemed to go on forever. They had a pool, a volleyball court and a field where we played touch football. They grew their own vegetables and had fruit trees. Due to the building development on Staten Island their yard now only extends twenty feet beyond the house. There was an Irish folk band there that day which gave the party a festive flavor. One of the band members, a banjo player, asked me what I was using. He had seen me open some tin foil and bite off a brown plug. I told him I had gotten it in Colorado and it was real strong shit. I assumed he knew it was legal chewing tobacco. He actually thought it was a controlled substance. I gave him a piece, which he smelled, squeezed, and tasted with just the tip of his tongue. I told him to keep it between his inner cheek and gum and not to swallow the juice but spit it out. He took it, thanked me profusely with a thick Irish brogue and proceeded to get very, very stoned. When he played his banjo on the next set he did things with his fingers he had never done before. After I had gone, I was told he was looking all over for me to score more "stuff." To this day, I will bet there is a group of musicians in Ireland who believe there is a plant that grows in Colorado with magical, talent-enhancing properties.

Now that I am older and have become aware of the health risks associated with tobacco, I use another method to keep me alert on the highway. I constantly drink water so that I am encouraged, by bodily urges, to make frequent stops. About every hundred miles I hit either a rest stop or a gas station. I always park a distance from the rest room so I walk a bit longer for needed and stimulating exercise. I find that this helps greatly to maintain alertness on the highway.

CHAPTER 4

Big Momma

Donna Freeland has large prominent breasts. Her boy-friend Pete refers to her as, Big Momma from New York. She is a friendly, witty, outgoing sort. Big Momma is a psychiatric nurse who works with addicts. "Not just the street, urine-stained sad types but many successful professionals too," she indicated as she sped through her small but efficient kitchen preparing hors d' oeuvres.

She has been divorced twice, both marriages to Jewish men. Unhappy over the relationships with each of these former husbands, Donna loudly proclaimed, "From now on, when I date men I make sure their foreskins are intact."

Donna also indicated that when she drinks a bit she becomes quite uninhibited. Without even taking a drink, after a large seven-course dinner, she insisted that she is extremely talented in giving oral pleasure. She then emphasized, "I am good at it, I mean, really good at it." She said the last time she was in a restaurant she demonstrated her manual technique for self-arousal. She said she used a spoon. I'm glad I wasn't there.

Donna loves food and all its affections. She enjoyed talking about what she was going to prepare. She was so thrilled in planning the dinner party for Pete and his two friends. She was excited at every aspect that evolved around the food, drink, and the possibility of sex. She took Pete, Fred Stephens and me food shopping. We went all the way to Littleton, a 30 minute drive, so she could purchase some specialty items there. Pete couldn't understand why she didn't shop around the corner at Albertson's. "You aren't from New York, you will never understand," she replied.

She had to have four different meats. There was a London broil, lamb chops, a boned chicken, and an Italian sausage. The sausage was the kind that is rolled in a 12-inch wheel flavored with cheese and herbs with a thin stake securing it.

There were four vegetables in addition to the salad. The artichokes were drenched with garlic butter and the asparagus was dressed with a hollandaise sauce. She made the sauce herself.

The dinner was accompanied by Cabernet Sauvignon and finished off with espresso. For desert there was peach pie a la mode and baklava.

When one of the guests suggested, "Let's have an orgy," she stopped talking, looked into his eyes and waited with great expectation at what he would say next. He stood mute. There was no orgy, he was just kidding. She displayed visible disappointment when conversation on the subject was dropped. When Pete put a soft porn movie on cable she thought there would be something to stimulate the conversation back to an orgy mode. Sadly, again she was disappointed. The three men were so worn out from the meal she realized little could be done to sway them. She wondered later if she should have tried harder. She brought out the Polaroid camera and thought about removing her top for pictures but did not. Little did she know that all three men in the room were also disappointed.

It was clear that Donna had a food disorder. Her kitchen though, had a furniture disorder. The corners of the room were stacked with food and soda. Kitchen tools were everywhere and so were boxes of snacks. Potato chips, Doritos, cookies, nuts, and clearly, all snacking items were kept within easy reach.

Several weeks after this was written in August 1999, Donna was fired from her job. She had mentioned that her boss was a witch. Donna also suffered an emotional trauma when her twenty-something son was hospitalized for drug abuse. She since has allowed her son, who was on probation for an unmentioned crime, to move in with her. Pete expressed sympathy for her.

♪♪♪

Pete and Fred were newly retired employees from a U.S. government agency. It was an agency whose function is to gather intelligence and information concerning individuals, organizations and foreign countries who pose a threat to the United States. Pete celebrates his birthday every year by inviting all his former USMC and colleagues to a golf tournament and a pig roast at his house. It is always attended by scores of friends.

A few years ago Fred and I arrived several days ahead of the other attendees and we had a memorable visit to The Stanley Hotel in Estes Park. I had spent a wonderful vacation there several years earlier with my second wife Carole Pilling. Since it was a mere half hour drive from Pete's house, we made the hop.

Pete at the Stanley Hotel. Estes Park, CO.

CHAPTER **5**

Biker Brothers

It's still 1999 and I am homeward-bound. As I listen to Willie sing *Angels Flying too Close to the Ground,* I cross the Missouri River and enter Council Bluffs, Iowa. This is always a stop for me. There is a huge shopping center at Exit 5, five miles east of the Missouri River. An excellent supermarket with deli section that makes sandwiches to go is called the Hi Vee and located there. I believe there is a chain of them here in the west. I buy sandwiches and fried chicken with a fruit salad from their salad bar for my long ride into Nebraska. When traveling these long distances, I constantly set short-term goals. The Hi Vee in Council Bluffs is always a welcome stop.

There will be no stop for me now because I am heading home and it is evening rush hour. This factor makes me dedicated to passing through here as quickly as possible. My goal is to pass Des Moines and spend the night a bit east of it. A bit is measured by how I feel at the time.

I am now seeing more motorcycles on the road. They are highway rovers who have been to the rally at Sturgis,

ND and are leaving early to beat the crowds. On my way out west, I spoke to several groups of these riders. They had traveled long distances to get to Sturgis. When they cast an envious eye on my new Road King they always asked, "Hey man, are you going to Sturgis?" At first I explained I was going to South Park, Colorado to ride in a parade. Then their curiosity forced them to ask if it was the same place as the cable TV adult cartoon episodes. When the explanation got too lengthy, I was in a hurry; I always am when heading west, I just answered, "Yea, man."

I do not see any bikes heading west. The Sturgis rally is just about ending. There is no reason for bikers to drive west now. It is beginning to rain and my sympathy is with these bikers for they have many miles to travel on just two wheels. There is just a matter of inches between them and the highway that is rushing past the soles of their boots at 75 mph. A piece of debris on the road, a wet patch or an exit ramp with changing angles, can cause a skid that can easily cause the bike to go down. The biker has to keep both hands on the grips constantly, his eyes must remain to the direct front and alertness must be never-ending. There is little time to relax. In traffic relaxation time on a bike is never. An automobile driver can avert his eyes from the road, he can shift his body in the seat, he can blow his nose, adjust his testicles, and he can eat a sandwich or drink from a water bottle. A biker cannot afford such luxuries. He cannot look at the regal raptor gliding on wind currents overhead nor can he reach for a tissue. He cannot even afford to sneeze. He has to sit on his balls and cut off the blood circulation to them. The snot drips from his nose unimpeded. He gets hungry, thirsty and can only check out the cute female driver he is passing for a brief instant.

There are many sacrifices a biker must make. He must be disciplined, he must maintain his balance, and his head must remain upright, because tilting the head causes a loss of balance that could be disastrous. When a motorcyclist drops his bike at highway speeds, the rider had better be wearing boots and leather pants, jacket and full fingered gloves. Going down on a bike at highway speeds can cause anything from road rash abrasions, to death if the rider ends up under the wheels of another vehicle.

I have gone down twice. It was an experience of pure terror. The first time was at 40 mph when a driver abruptly shifted lanes. The bozo accelerated into my lane and in doing so struck the front wheel of my bike. The impact caused me to land on my left side with the bike lying on my left leg. Because I was not wearing boots, the grinding to a stop sandpapered the skin off my left ankle down to the bone. Since traffic was able to stop behind me, I was fortunate that I was not run over by oncoming vehicles.

♪♪♪♫

The other time I hit the pavement occurred while taking a left turn on a new bike I had just purchased. I was riding home from the showroom. I had been used to leaning into a wide turn near my house with my previous bike, a 1965 chopped 650cc Triumph. This new 1980 650cc Honda was engineered differently and down I went at about 25 mph. I had no injuries, I was wearing proper clothing. It did scare the shit out of me though. Steve Kelly, who was driving my van behind me, couldn't stop laughing. I am glad he was there so I could laugh too. Steve's laughter, I knew from past experience, had a way of making pain go away.

At the age of 50, in January 2005 Steve died of cancer. Those who knew him always thought his end would come in a quick, thunderous or violent manner. The same way he lived! For Steve to succumb to the slow ravages of cancer was not commensurate with his life. His comfort came from being cared for and surrounded by a loving

Steve Kelly

wife, son, family and friends.

In the late 1970's, Steve talked me into entering a rodeo to ride in the bareback bronco competition. My ride lasted about two seconds but the memories of that day will last many of us a lifetime. Steve won the bull riding competition that day. He was an avid motorcycle rider, referring to his Harley as his iron horse. Steve was affectionate and had the biggest of hearts. He had so many friends; there was no room at the funeral home due to the huge crowds that came to mourn him. He owned a welding company at his time of death and left his loving wife Carmela, a son Steve, his parents, George and Clare, and brothers, Kevin, Brian, and Mark. He also left sisters Christine, Janet and Mary Beth. I consider all of his family among my closest friends. Those who knew Steve never thought his death would come in such a slow, agonizing fashion. It was not a fitting end for someone who lived such a fast, dangerous and exciting life.

The following is the news article that was in the November 27, 1978 issue of the *Staten Island Advance:*

<u>Sport Scene</u>
Pupil takes ex-coach for a ride
By JACK MINOGUE

Steve Kelly can still remember the feeling. There he was, a guy who had run the route of rodeo events from bronc riding to bull-dogging with nothing but confidence, but now he had that queasy feeling in the pit of his stomach. "There was always a kind of respect that went with rodeo events," he said, "but I had been doing that kind of thing since I was 11 or 12 living across from-and spending most of my time-in the stables on Willowbrook Road."

But as a senior at Susan E. Wagner High School he decided to get into something "a little different" and answered the call when Alex Flint founded the school's gymnastic team.

"Now that," Kelly said, "was scary." When Alex had me doing those double-back somersaults on the trampoline, I

always had the feeling I was going to miss everything and land on the floor."

Kelly, who did some riding on the pro circuit after leaving Susan Wagner, had an opportunity to turn the tables on his old coach just before the start of gymnastics.

"Steve got away from rodeos for a while," Alex explained, "but now he is back into it-and he dragged me along with him. He's coaching me like I used to coach him."

Kelly conned Alex into trying his hand at bronc riding, a sport that reminds Flint a little of gymnastics. "It's not just how long you're up," Flint said. "I learned that your form has much to do with the scoring. Which is how it is in gymnastics."

Like Kelly, the gymnast, bronc rider Alex Flint is not worried about the time he's on the horse's back. "I'm told that the eight seconds you're expected to stay on seems like eight years," Flint laughed, "but that's OK. Hitting the ground is my big concern. If I know when I'm getting off, that's OK because I know I'll be able to land on my feet. Unfortunately, the horse doesn't give advance notice."

Which is exactly what happened on Flint's debut.

Competing in the Abilene Stables' rodeo, Alex drew the toughest horse in the field for his bow which this horse unceremoniously cut short after three seconds.

"Well, I've got a little pain in my left hip and my right cheek hurts when I sit down, but I can still walk, so I guess everything is alright," Flint kidded that day.

But I don't think I'll try that again for some time...not until the weather warms up and the ground softens. "Until then, I'll concentrate on coaching gymnastics and skiing. Which reminds me, Hey Steve!" he called, as Kelly edged toward the door.

〉〉〉〉

The Thanksgiving of 1976 was my worst and yet in a way, it was my best. It was my first Thanksgiving not being part of my family. Awkward is not the right term to use to describe it. It is not painful enough. There existed a loneliness that is indescribable. I remember it well when Clare invited me to that Kelly Thanksgiving. It was that invitation and attending of that well planned dinner, which formed within me a sense of growth and acceptance of my new identity.

My parents were in Florida and I could have spent the holiday with any of my cousins but I chose to accept the invitation of the Kelly family. The sympathy and sadness from my family members would have been a real bummer for me. George and Clare Kelly, with whom I became good friends, were parents of former students of mine. Steve and Mark in 1971 were members of my fledgling gymnastic team. A few years later Mary Beth was to be a member of my physical education yoga class. They were a pleasure to be around. I loved them all then and now, thirty-four years later, still do today.

Steve had won a cabin cruiser in a card game. The boat was in rough shape. It was an old wooden, 30-foot lapstrake-sided cabin boat that Steve had towed to his parent's back yard. Along with dozens of Steve's friends, we worked to make it seaworthy. That meant that the dry, old-fashioned creosote rope caulk that was stuffed in the seams had to be scraped off, pulled out and replaced with new caulk. In addition, the boat was sanded, and sanded and then sanded a bit more. Then the boat was liberally smeared with paint and polyutherene. All these hours of work took place in a festive atmosphere over many afternoons and weekends and cases of beer. Steve's vibrant personality created a party atmosphere; it always did. His persona was evidenced by his naming the boat *Sin or Swim*.

When spring came around the boat had a docking space in Great Kills Harbor. One afternoon, along with Kenny Quin and Steve, the three of us took the maiden voyage. The engine conked out twice but the engine gremlins were no match for Steve and Kenny's masterful mechanical skills. The boat was soon cutting through the light chop of Raritan Bay. When we got to the Verrazano Bridge, Steve fell overboard. I'm not sure what he was reaching for or how he slipped but I do remember laughing so hard that I cried, I mean I really cried. Tears were rolling down my face, for sure. Besides the beer that was available for quenching our thirst on that cool day, I only remember the laughter. I am not sure who was laughing the most, Kenny, me, or Steve as I hauled him out of the water.

The afternoon wasn't over; we still had to get back to the harbor. There was more laughter to come. It seems Steve would not be the only one in the water that cool spring day. As we got back to the dock, Steve piloted the *Sin or Swim* toward the direction of our berth, our speed was slowed by side swiping a docked boat. As we approached our slip, Kenny reached for the overhead steel strand wire to connect to the stern of the boat. Somehow, and I don't know why I can't remember, the boat moved away from the overhead wire but Kenny was still holding on to it. Try to picture Kenny loudly protesting to Steve to slow the boat as it passed away from him. Kenny remained holding on to the wire and nothing was under him but cold harbor water. The boat soon struck the wall of the dock like a typical Staten Island ferryboat enacting its docking procedure. The *Sin or Swim* then careened into a conveniently empty boat anchored nearby. While this was happening we were about twenty feet away from Ken who was hanging on to the thin steel strand wire and the distance was widening. Kenny must have felt that if he yelled louder it would somehow give Steve miraculous powers to reverse the boat as he would a car. Well we learned a valuable lesson that day that boats cannot be parked like cars. There are no brakes. We were only able to slow down by hitting into things. Among them were pilings, docks and other boats which numbered four, at least.

My memory is a bit foggy here but I distinctly remember hearing the loudest exclamation of, "Oh shit" just before Kenny hit the cold water.

With the aid of the aforementioned objects, as a dripping Ken scrambled up the pier wall, Steve was able to get the boat into the vicinity of the hanging wire and we were able to secure the boat in its proper dock.

The next day we couldn't wait to get to the boat to practice our newly learned piloting skills. We discussed how there were no brakes like a car and reversing the engines must be the way to slow down the boat. Issuing us the challenge, the *Sin or Swim* beckoned us to the harbor. After parking the car, hoisting the beer chest from the trunk, we made our way to the dock. In complete silence we pondered with surprise and shock the view in front of us. All we could see of the *Sin or Swim* was the cabin roof and the radio antenna. The remainder of the *Sin or Swim* lay serenely on the bottom. It seemed all that caulking, sanding, and polyutherene did little good.

I don't remember whatever became of the *Sin or Swim*; again my memory is foggy here. It may still be resting at the bottom of Great Kills Harbor.

A helmet is considered the most important piece of motorcycle safety equipment and is mandatory in most states. There are states that do not have mandatory helmet laws. A certain group of bikers believe so much in the freedom of choice, that they have chosen to make their residence in those states. Colorado is a helmet free state. There are many motorcyclists who have chosen to live, work, and raise their families there for just that reason. There was a group of bikers I spoke to in Longmont, Colorado that was card-carrying members of the Libertarian Party. Howard Stern, the radio personality once, was the gubernatorial candidate from New York for the Libertarian Party. The parties' tenet is freedom from excessive governmental control. Their platform includes, removing the ban on prostitution, chemical substances and that all drugs should be treated the same as alcohol. They also believe strongly in the Second Amendment rights and the freedom to bear arms. They believe in a woman's right to an abortion without government subsidies, but primary on the mind of these Coloradoans is the freedom to ride a motorcycle without having to wear a helmet.

On my trip west this year in my 1999 Lincoln Continental with trailer hitch attached, connected to a MYCO motorcycle trailer with my 1999 Harley Davidson Road King

Classic with wide white wall tires, I forgot to bring my helmet. I am used to wearing a helmet when I ride and felt vulnerable without one. So I went to the Harley dealer in Longmont to purchase one. When I asked to see his selection, I was strongly answered by the manager, "Hell we don't sell helmets here. We don't even allow them inside this place." We fight hard enough to keep helmet legislation from becoming enacted."

I never realized the emotion that was attached to helmets. A few weeks earlier, I had completed an interactive three-day motorcycle safety course sponsored by the American Motorcycle Association. New York State waives the taking of a riding test to grant a motorcycle license if this course is successfully completed. It was an excellent course in which, after riding for 40 years taught me much I did not know. The most memorable safety point that was impressed upon the class of 15 was that a helmet is a necessary part of a biker's apparel. To bring home this point, we were shown photos of head injuries. I was convinced. I chose to wear a helmet. I also believe though, that as in guns, drugs, and abortions, that the individual should

Dad on his 1932 AJS Racing Motorcycle

have the right to choose and too much government is detrimental. Freedom from excessive governmental control and taxation is why our forefathers fought a war against the British. Many Americans have forgotten that we won that war.

$$\smile\smile\smile$$

I am getting fatigued now as I approach Des Moines. The ground is wet from the light rain and it is getting dark. A tractor-trailer passes me creating a heavy mist in its wake. There are three lowrider Harleys that are riding the slipstream of the huge truck. They are free from the rain because of the vacuum created by the goliath vehicle but cannot see anything in front of them except the rear wall of truck they are behind. I feel a twinge of sympathy for my biker brothers because I know they are far from relaxed. The only reaction they can make is related to the tail light of the truck they are following. They cannot see anything else on the road. I would never have the nerve to perform such a dangerous stunt. Those are three brave dudes. They may be heading for Chicago, a grueling seven hours away. They have already been riding for 12 hours and I know they are tired. Other riders I meet at a rest stop are heading for Cleveland; they have twice that, 14 hours to go. I hope, like me in my comfortable Lincoln, they are planning to stop for the night. It is eight o' clock in the evening now and these dudes left Sturgis after breakfast at nine o'clock this morning. I feel sorry for these bikers and say a silent prayer for them because I know they are tense, tired and scared.

Now, I am really getting fatigued. I have been driving

a bit longer than these bikers. My mileage distance from Salida is longer than theirs from Sturgis. I have the luxury of sitting in a comfortable car, listening to my favorite music, reaching in my small ice chest for a peanut butter sandwich, I have had five so far, and a cool bottle of Starbuck's Cappuccino when ever the urge strikes me. The motorcycle riders on this Interstate who are all around me cannot relax like this. As the exhaustion sets in, I decide to pull off at Newton, which is about a half-hour past Des Moines. There are seven motels at this stop and I feel confident I will get a room. I am so wrong. I am so absolutely frigging wrong. The Iowa State Fair is going on and the rooms have been held in reserve since last year's fair. The young girl behind the desk, after telling me of the room situation, asks if I want to reserve one for next year because there is a waiting list. Duh! The leather belt I am wearing is older than she is and I tell her I need time to think about it. I am tired and disappointed and get back on the interstate heading east. I see more bikers and think of how fatigued they must be. I have a seven-way power seat with an electric lumbar support in my hot rod Lincoln. The bikers have no such electric luxuries. The poor guys I see have no back support. Now I really feel bad for my biker brothers.

I pull off the highway at Grinnell about 30 miles to the east, still no room at the Inn. I am now more tired and disappointed. I wish now I had my black Darth Vader van so I could sleep in relative comfort during an emergency like this. It is back on the Interstate and eastward into the dark wet night. 30 more miles to Williamsburg Iowa and I stop at the Ramada Inn I stayed at on the way West three weeks ago. It is 10:30 and I am so tired I hit the sheets without a shower.

I awake at four am, I bring my body to life in a hot shower and continue eastward on a wet highway. The rain has stopped and I hope for a dry day. I am immune from the weather in my silver jewel Lincoln but I am concerned for the bikers on their way home from Sturgis. There are still a few on the road and I am concerned for them because the weather report promises thunderstorms all day.

This year, 1999 was a special adventure because I got to experience Harley adventures. One of them took place in Hartsel, CO which is located in South Park. That was the year I was asked to participate in the Hartsel Days celebration. The editor of the *South Park Palladium* asked me to write of my impressions of her beautiful town. The following is what was published in the September 1999 issue.

NEW YORKER TAKES HOME A BIT OF SOUTH PARK

Editor's note: Alexander Flint of Staten Island, NY, has been an annual visitor to Colorado for many years. This summer he made a special stop in beautiful downtown Hartsel during the year's celebration of Hartsel Days riding his new Harley in the parade and meeting some of the townsfolk. Here are his impressions:

SOUTH PARK, COLORADO —

"Hey! Are you going to Sturgis?" Every stop I made along Interstate 80 while traveling from my home in Staten Island to South Park, CO, I was asked that question. The new Harley Davidson Road King Classic I was pulling in a

motorcycle trailer identified me as a select group of in-dividuals. When I purchased the machine from Lombardi and Sons in my hometown, I was automatically enrolled as a member of H.O.G., an acronym for Harley Owners Group.

I didn't think much of the biker identity until I was re-peatedly asked the same question. Referring, of course, to Sturgis, SD, the site in the Black Hills of one of the larg-est motorcycle rallies, which was due to start the following week.

My answer was always the same: "No, I'm going to South Park, CO."

"You mean, like the TV show?"

"Yeah, the same place," I would answer and smile. I always got a funny look in response to my answer, but I left many inquisitors wondering if I was for real.

I was for real--- actually I was invited to ride my new motorcycle in the Hartsel Days parade, located in South Park.

I never got used to the bike trailer. I would look in the rearview mirror whenever the need arose and was always shocked by the appearance of an impatient, tailgating Harley. It fooled me every time. Once at a rest stop, I got out of the car and for an instant, I wondered who could be so lucky as to own that beautiful molded chrome and shiny work of art that was parked behind me.

The instant would pass, and with a touch of embarrass-ment, I realized it was mine.

My first stop in Colorado was in Longmont, a growing city just outside of Boulder. Since the bike was brand new-only 200 miles on it-I had put on a few hundred miles so I could get it serviced and considered it 'broken in.' And, the *servicing had to be done by a Harley dealer, to maintain the integrity of my one-year warranty, so I had put on at least 300 miles before venturing into the "wilds" of South Park.*

A few trips to Estes Park and a level ride to Loveland and the miles were there. After servicing in Longmont, I was on my way again.

I arranged with Kathleen Thomas, editor of the South Park Palladium, to meet at the HOB, the only bar in Hartsel and located in the center of town. The town consists of five buildings on either side of U.S. 24.

Not knowing what to expect, I was eager to meet Kathleen to show me where the parade was going to form up.

I was there in time for the pancake breakfast at the Hartsel fire station. The breakfast I had of pancakes, orange juice and coffee was great, but the biggest surprise I had was the professionalism of the Rescue Squad.

They gave a demonstration using various tools of rescue, including the" Jaws of Life," to dismantle a car in almost no time at all, the object being to extract injured occupants so they could receive medical attention. The squad, at a recent competition in Colorado Springs finished fifth place out of a field of hundreds of entries. They are a proud and well-trained group of professionals.

The parade, also known as the Shortest Parade in History, "was pure fun." It was the first parade I participated in since my graduation parade from The USMC Basic School in Quantico, VA., which marked the beginning of my military reserve career in the 1960's.

Among the Hartsel parade participants was a handful of armed U.S. Army Horse Soldiers circa 1800's, accompanied by an Indian scout. An authentic Sheriff's Posse was present, and from the look of those officers I believe a fugitive would stand a better chance of escaping the Texas Rangers.

There was a fully restored 1947 maroon Ford pickup truck, and I cannot remember seeing a better paint job on any vehicle. There were other pickup trucks-I mean many pickup trucks.

I saw more pickup trucks that morning than, I believe, I have ever seen in one place in all of New York City. And it seemed that every truck was accompanied by a dog.

Unlike New York City animals, these dogs roamed loose when out of the truck and, like their owners, were well mannered. New York has leash and pick-up laws.

When I walk Ava, my Rottweiler, twice a day, I travel armed with a pocket full of plastic bags. I have never been mugged back home, in fact the bad guys cross the street when they see me coming.

Now that I mention it, most people cross the street when we approach. Sometimes mothers run from their houses to retrieve their children when they see us turn the corner.

But in Hartsel, this dog fear was nonexistent. Instead, there was a sense of harmony among man and beast that beautiful, sunny, blue-skied morning.

Several fire fighting vehicles were also in the parade, quite visible as they sprayed water almost as high as the sky. And they were audible, very audible.

The traffic on U.S. 24 was closed in both directions while the parade passed in front of the HOB and then turned back off the highway.

There were numerous cowboy-attired horseback riders, and a Tom Mix-era cowboy. Duley Canterbury actually punched cows when all silver screen cowboys wore spurs. I was told Duley was in his 80's although from the robust physical appearance he gave, I found that hard to believe.

When he stopped at the HOB for a drink, he was asked, "Duley, would you like a Bloody Mary?" His prompt reply was, "whose Mary?"

I was also impressed with Violet, the owner of the HOB, an acronym, which stands for, Hateful Old Bitch. She spoke with a lingo suggestive of a Brooklyn longshoreman but also displayed benevolence reminiscent of Mother Teresa.

One of these aspects of Vi's personality was highlighted by the discussion of the previous night's frolic in the HOB. It seems there was dancing on the table, and Vi said that such behavior was not tolerated in the HOB.

Vi also explained the "86 board" to me. It's a handprinted board, prominently displayed above the bar, with names of individuals who are forevermore banned from the HOB.

The HOB itself was quite interesting, with walls adorned with numerous signs. Among them was the philosophical statement, "Never climb a barbed wire fence naked," and "Life is too short to dance with ugly men."

I have been frequenting bars in New York City for many years, and I can say I never have seen any notation more poignant than these.

I greatly enjoyed Hartsel Days, its parade and residents, and felt an almost surreal atmosphere surrounding me. The vintage, well cared for, pickup trucks; the people dressed from eras gone by, the cowboy with a hand-tooled belt with the words, "dirty belt" embossed on it-the mix of old and new was evident everywhere.

A modern CD jukebox with Grateful Dead albums in the HOB, townspeople armed with both cell phones and western style Colt pistols in leather holsters and vehicles that were old when I was a child all blended to give me an experience that could be found nowhere in New York City.

I will be back sometime next year.

As I mounted my Harley to leave, someone called out, "Hey man, are you going to Sturgis?"

I smiled and answered, "Yeah, sooner or later."

❧❧❧❧

In October 1999, the *Staten Island Advance* also carried a story on my trip to South Park.

RETIRED TEACHER GETS TASTE OF THE REAL SOUTH PARK

ALEX FLINT FINDS THAT THE COLORADO COUNTY IS A TREASURED VACATION SPOT, AS WELL AS A STEP BACK IN TIME.

By Tamara Valles
Staten Island Advance October 24, 1999

Park County, a large rural region in the center of Colorado, home to thousands of miles of open pasture, old western-style saloons, mountain lions and pistol carrying cowboys-has proved to be the perfect vacation getaway for New Dorp resident Alexander Flint for the last 21 years.

This past summer, Flint, a grandfather of four and retired physical education teacher and coach at Susan E. Wagner High School, spent three weeks mountain biking through a small part of the region known as South Park.

That's right, South Park-as in the TV cartoon show.

"Except the characters are far, far beyond what the cartoon depicts," Flint said.

Flint and his brand new-Harley Davidson, which he brought along in a trailer attached to his Lincoln Continental, were invited to ride in the county's annual Hartsel Days Parade.

"Among the participants were a handful of armed U.S. Army horse soldiers from the 1800s, accompanied by an Indian scout. An authentic sheriff was present-and from the look of those officers, I believe a fugitive would stand a better chance of escaping the Texas Rangers," Flint noted.

But the region's uniqueness lies in the fact that these are not actors in costume; scenes like this are the everyday norm in South Park.

This pristine countryside, home to about 5,000 residents, is more than just a treasured vacation spot for Flint-it's a step back in time.

It's not uncommon, for example, to see shepherds gathered, guarding their sheep against wolves-a scene which Flint describes as reminiscent more of biblical times than modern-day America.

In addition, private telephone lines have only existed there since the early 1990's. Before that time, multiple residents shared one phone line.

Flint explained that on a typical day in South Park, visitors will find scores of well-mannered dogs roaming the dirt roads side-by-side with friendly townsfolk dressed in clothing from eras gone by-a far cry from the trendy city-folk that Flint usually encounters here on the Island.

But residents of this primitive region appear to blend the old with the new.

"I felt an almost surreal atmosphere surrounding me. Townspeople are armed with both cell phones and Western-style Colt pistols in leather holsters drive vehicles that were old when I was a child," Flint said.

Park County hasn't changed much in the past 100 years, but according to Flint, newcomers wielding new technological advances are presently attempting to encroach upon the area-much to the dismay of the residents.

There is less land for its native wildlife-which include antelope, bison, black bears and coyotes-and more and more people are moving in-people wish to impose city-like restrictions on this peaceful mountainside community.

These new residents want more and more police officers, traffic lights and sidewalks. Some developers even want to break up old family-run ranches.

The 27,000-acre Hartsel Ranch, for example, was sold recently and residents fear that it will be subdivided into 35-acre parcels, which would clearly threaten its long-preserved historical integrity.

"The old ways are being forced out," Flint noted with a twinge of sadness in his voice. "These developers are part of the evil empire that wants to take nature away," he added.

But residents of Park County and South Park in particular are fighting-and so far, they're winning.

Kathleen Thomas, president of the South Park Chamber of Commerce and editor of the South Park Palladium, is happy to report that "no major developments have been approved by the county government yet."

South Park is still an ideal destination for those, like Flint, who desire peace and quiet, a taste of rugged beauty and a little old-fashioned hospitality.

"I'll definitely be back next year," Flint said.

My 1999 Harley Davidson Road King Classic

CHAPTER 6

Highway Madness

It is a wet highway as I continue my drive home. I am beginning the second day as I roll over the wet highway and I wonder if I will have the energy to continue without sleep all the way to Staten Island. As I listen to Willie Nelson sing *Faded Love*, I am somehow motivated in my drive. The entire trip entails 36 hours of driving. So far I have traveled 18 hours, almost half way. In 1980, which was the third year of this obsessive continuous streak of travel between Staten Island and Colorado, I drove home with Alex nonstop. That's right; I did not stop to sleep. It was a crazy thing to do but I was younger and dumber back then. I endured 36 hours of continuous driving. I thought I could alternate between radio stations, cassettes, (there were no CD's, Walkmans or IPods in 1979) the CB radio and conversation with other road rovers to keep myself sharp.

I vowed never to do it again. I thought I was invincible and did not have to follow the rules of rest. I was so wrong! By the time I reached New Jersey on that marathon drive, I began to hallucinate. I had been driving for 34 hours when

I saw the first praying mantis on the side of the highway.

Now, I know what you are thinking! How could someone driving on a highway see a small insect on the side of the road unless he had superhuman vision? Right? Wrong! The bug was easy to see because it was the size of a football field. First, I mistook the monster apparition for a battleship. But I was so wrong, once I got a better look at it. Clearly, it was a praying mantis.

I don't know what caused the phantom to appear. First I thought it was due to some chewing tobacco juice I may have swallowed. Then I thought it was due too much black coffee. But after reading of some of the Native American rituals of initiation, as in *A Man Called Horse*, clearly it was due to sleep deprivation. It would be safe to say that along with my judgment, my vision was also impaired. I realized too, my reasoning process was compromised and could not make the proper decision to stop for the night. I reasoned at that point in New Jersey, I was only one hour from home; therefore I was too close to stop to spend the night. Actually I was underestimating; I really was two hours away from my home in New Dorp, Staten Island.

I should have realized that six hours earlier in Pennsylvania I was in trouble when I entered a panic mode. I had stopped at an all-night burger joint to use the toilet facilities and immediately hopped back in the van to continue the eastward march. Alex was sleeping in the rear sofabed in the van when I made the stop. About an hour later I had the terrifying thought, "What if Alex followed me in and was in the bathroom when I drove off?" Immediately, I snapped on the interior lights. Looking over my shoulder to check on him, all I could see was a jumble of laundry, sleeping bags and pillows. There was no sign of Alex. My first impulse was to hit the brakes, pull over, and stop to check. If I did, I could have caused a serious accident, so I had to wait for a safe area to stop. The next few minutes, while looking for that safe place to stop were pure terror for me. I could only think of an eight-year old boy frightened, lost and alone in a strange restaurant, in an unknown location. I didn't want to call out to him and wake him up because I thought if I called out and he didn't answer my fears would be confirmed. I considered driving across the median and heading back in a westerly direction even before I confirmed him to be missing. Fortunately there was a wide shoulder that appeared ahead and I pulled over on it. My climbing out of the front seat and making my way to the jumbled pile of blankets was the most fearful moment of my 39 year old life. The sight of his mass of long blond hair was the prettiest sight I had ever seen. Holy shit, he was there!

I should have looked for a place to sleep then, but I was adrenalized and was a driven madman who could only think of maintaining an eastward motion on Interstate 80, and home. I am not sure what this intense obsession to return home was caused by then. In retrospect, I believe it was to gather with and nurture my other children. Like a wild canine driven to return to his pack. The concept of being a single father was still fairly new. It had been four years since Irene and I had separated and I still could not accept or understand it. I was still unable to recognize my new identity as a single parent. That wasn't how I saw myself. I only recognized a family as having parents and children living together. This single life was a situation I didn't want or comprehend.

In the spring of 1976, after 16 years of marriage and five kids, Irene informed me one day, as I arrived home from school, she wanted a divorce. At first I thought she was kidding. I laughed at first, thinking she had a bad day with the kids; she wasn't kidding, and she was quite serious. When the reality of her decision hit me, I was shocked, dumbfounded, and nearly destroyed. I didn't consider myself a bad husband or father. I could have, in fact, been considered a model husband and father. I was not a drunk, I didn't gamble, and I never had an involvement with another woman. At the time of our marriage I was in fact, a virgin. We both were. We were barely out of our teens when we were married. I was a model husband/ father. Unfortunately at the time, Irene did not think of me as a model anything. My self-esteem quickly dwindled and soon became nonexistent.

I was in a total state of shock. I was bewildered, baffled and confused. I was without a clue as to which way to turn. When I was able to think more clearly, I offered to remain living with Irene and have us each live a separate life and maintain a home together for the sake of the children. Her father was the one to first offer that solution. Irene wanted no part of me though. Her only interest, it seemed to me at the time, was how much alimony I would pay her when I was out of the house. I then offered to remain with the kids because I was the one who wanted to keep the family intact, an offer I would repeat in the future. Irene though, would have none of it.

I did not want to leave. I wanted to remain in my home, with my family. Bob Donahue, the father of a great gymnast on my high school team, became my lawyer. Bob informed me that no judge in the country would grant me the house and kids. It was not acceptable for a father in my situation to be granted custody. It could only occur; I was informed, in the case of an incompetent or criminal mother. That was not the case. Irene was quite competent and she was no criminal. The kids I love so much, the kids I wanted to spend all my fun time with, the Victorian house I lovingly worked to restore to its original appearance, was no longer to be my home. I felt great despair. I didn't know which way to turn.

The first insecurity I felt was in my manhood. I felt I was not good enough as a lover to my wife so she found some-one who was better. I had to find out if my sexual prowess was lacking. How was I to know? I was 37 years-old and had experienced only one sex partner my entire life. My wife! I unconsciously concluded that another woman was the immediate answer for me. I was teaching evening classes to adults and the first wide eyes that were flashed at me were from a beautiful divorcee, who was also a teacher. I called Helen and she was quite receptive. Wow! Life was about to pick up a whole lot. So it seemed.

☽☽☽☾

In that spring of 1976, once I realized the reality of my separation, I tried to read every book on the subject of divorce. Those books mostly directed the reader to think of himself. "Live your own life, be your own person" seemed to be the mantra. I thought that as selfish and was not me. I could only think of the five young lives who were more bewildered than me. I was determined to devote all the time I could to my children. I did have girlfriends; they were all younger than me, all attractive and all quite energetic. What they all seemed to have in common was to want their own family. I was not willing to accept the role of being a parent for a second family. I was only concerned with my five children. My devotion was to them.

The first weekend that came about, I began a ritual of living socially with my children. I took them to the movies, to rock concerts, to museums, skiing, and to the gymnastics summer camp. I wanted to be Super Dad!

I remember for the first few months buying six tickets to the Friday night movies in various theaters. The first movie we saw was *Carrie*, where Sissy Spacek played the part of a teenage girl under severe emotional stress. The kids liked it, maybe because they identified with that lost teen character in the movie. I'm sure it was because they too were under emotional stress.

After a few weeks, Nancy, who was 15 and the oldest, was drawn to her own social world, with friends her age. There were now only five tickets for me to buy. A week later, Eva also, begged out of our family entertainment time. Only four tickets to buy now. After about six months, Betsy was the next to leave my unraveling paternal nest. Three of us, me along with Alex and Debbie lasted about two years as a trio before Debbie came of age. Then it was her time to fledge the nest. Now it was just Alex who spent weekends with me in my condo. This lasted for several pleasant years until he followed his natural instinct to be drawn to his own adolescent age group. All through this period, my mother maintained her Sunday Italian dinners. She needs to be credited as the glue that kept us together,

During those weekends, I remember the Saturday and Sunday morning breakfasts at the local pancake house on Staten Island. After eating, we would drive to the Canary Bird Farm on Englishtown Road, off Route 9. I had a breeding pair of zebra finches and it was a good excuse to take a pleasant drive and buy them bird seed.

Alex stayed with me on weekends and accompanied me on my summer trips West for the next seven years. At that time, the invisible magnet that draws children into adulthood began to pull him too. In 1984, I made my first trip to the Rocky Mountains alone. It was to be the first of many trips alone. That was the way it should be, every healthy living thing grows. My kids had grown, now it was time for me to grow too.

In the 1990's while acting as a ranch sitter for Arlene and Chuck Jensen, my kids were old enough to fly out there to help me on the ranch. They returned in later years with their friends, flying on their own, renting their own vans, and taking responsibility for themselves. At that time I was so proud of them. The fears I had during that horrible spring of 1976 of my kids suffering from our drastic change in status, went unfounded.

⤳⤳⤳⤶

My first relationship was with Helen who had recently returned from a western state and worked there to put her husband through medical school. As soon as he became a doctor, he dumped her. In addition, he left her with all his medical school bills. That was her sad story. I would soon learn there were many sad stories attached to the divorcees I would meet and be dating in the immediate future. We remained together for 12 weeks and she put me in touch with her therapists. They were a competent husband and wife team. I went to them for counseling for about three months and felt better; actually I believe I was cured of my depression. I believe that the self-esteem I was able to elevate through my teaching and coaching jobs is what pulled me through. At the same time, I never forgot I was a father and devoted every weekend with the kids. In addition, I was at the New Dorp house every day after school to provide a sense of home life. Irene was working in the city and didn't return home until evening. I didn't want the kids to feel abandoned. I didn't want to feel like I was abandoned.

In 1986, Irene remarried and I bought her half of the house from her. I moved from my condo and have been here ever since.

☽☽☽☾

During the summers of 1976 and 1977 I took a job at Woodward Gymnastics Camp near State College, PA. The kids each spent a part of their summers with me. They were able to meet a number of nationally ranked gymnasts. Nancy my oldest, worked there with me one summer and developed a friendship with Elizabeth, a nice girl from South America who was a camper there. Betsy caught the eye of Ann Carr, the 1976 NCAA National Floor Exercise Champion, as a potentially great vaulter. I was very proud of my children at the camp.

In addition to Steve Nunno, now a prominent personality who is the coach of 1992 Olympic gold medal winner, Shannon Miller, I also met the Gonzalez family from Puerto Rico. They were five boys and were accompanied by their beautiful, former beauty queen, mother, Alba. Those boys had great talent as gymnasts; Mario went on to become a national champion. Their talents were not limited to gymnastics. They were all part of a rock band and were quite good. The following Easter, of 1977, I was invited to

Puerto Rico as guests of Alba and her husband Dr. Antonio Gonzales, who was an anesthesiologist. Their beautiful home was in the Rio Piedres section of San Francisco, located near San Juan.

I brought my oldest daughter, Nancy with me to Puerto Rico; she was 16 and became great friends with Alba and the boys. While we were there, I was introduced to a number of the parents of gymnasts who attended the same gymnastic school with the Gonzalez boys. They were mostly businessmen and doctors.

I soon found out that I was to be forced to make a life-altering decision. This group of influential people was involved with the national gymnastics team of Puerto Rico. They were concerned about the upcoming Pan American Games in 1979. They wanted to import a coach with national experience from the mainland. They offered me the job. They asked what my salary as a New York City teacher was. I told them. They said they would double that salary if I accepted. I was stunned, surprised and flattered. I never expected this. They took me to a beautiful beach location west of San Juan called Isle Verde. There was a condominium near completion that seemed identical to the one I was living in New Springville, near the Staten Island Mall. The difference was that this condo overlooked the exotic Caribbean Sea.

I had some long and hard thinking to do. I left Puerto Rico and told these fine gentlemen I would let them know of my decision in a week. It was nice to be wanted by someone but I didn't need a week. I knew on the flight back to New York that accepting that job and all the excitement that accompanied it, would leave my five children without a large part of the parental support I knew they counted on every day. Would my absence make my children resent me and their mother for my leaving? I am sure it would have had a negative effect. There were enough obstacles in their paths as it was. If I moved to another country, with all its beauty and lovely climate I am sure I would have remarried and probably started another family. Even though I would have bolstered my sagging psyche with this achievement, it could have been a disastrous blow to my kids. Although I would achieve some moments of fame and a sense of prominence, I felt it was wrong for me. It would be a world away and create a great divide between me and my kids. They didn't deserve that.

I remained as a physical education teacher and gymnastics coach at Susan E. Wagner High School and remained close to my children. I know it was the right decision. I am happy I made it.

Father and Son,
Woodward Gymnastics Camp 1977

CHAPTER **7**

Autobahn Connection

As I continue my road march eastward into Illinois, I approach a junction on Interstate 80. Another interstate is heralded by huge white-on-green highway signs. A driver is given the option to veer southeastward to I-74 which leads to Peoria, the birthplace of my hero, former president Ronald Reagan, and beyond to Bloomington. I comfortably pass this fork and continue on toward Chicago.

For some reason, this junction, in this friendly, familiar United States setting, brings to mind a similar junction in a strange land far, far away. My memory is elicited by a song playing on the radio. It is the 1950s country song by Bobby Helms, *Fraulein*. It is a song that begins, *"Far across blue water lives an old German's daughter by the banks of the river Rhine."* This distant land offered a setting that was not at all familiar and sometimes not too friendly. Last fall, while driving through Europe, I would panic every time I was offered an option to leave the autobahn. Firstly, the cities offered as directions on the highway signs were totally unknown to me. Secondly, the fact that they were in another language tended to dampen my armpits a bit.

I remember the drive from Heidelberg, Germany to Amsterdam in Holland. I had to follow the autobahn A-61 in a Northeast direction to Venlo, Netherlands. This was to take me past Cologne, Germany, a city known for its 4711 perfume. A favorite of mine, 4711 has been around since 1873. A bit of terror occurred when Cologne did not appear on my map. How could the cologne still be here but the city disappear?

This caused a mild panic among the complexities of my digestive system. I asked directions at a rest stop. Now you have to understand these were not like our American rest stops. There were no toilets. There were just trees for men to stand behind. The men I saw just stood in the open to urinate. A truck driver who was helpful showed me that surely Cologne was on my map. Sure it was, right in front of my eyes, exactly where it was supposed to be, only it was spelled, Koln, with a two dot accent over the O. My confidence began quickly to erode. Perhaps I should have followed Liz Ryan's advice and taken the train. Liz was a beautiful American, a coworker at ODCSINT, the Office of the Deputy Chief of Staff Intelligence, who lived and worked in Heidelberg. She tried to dissuade me from the auto trip in favor of taking the train. I don't know why I didn't listen to Liz.

I drove past Koln, with the two dot accent over the O, and continued on to Venlo, Holland. Holland and The Netherlands are used interchangeably to identify this beautiful country. I don't know why there can't be one name for each country in the world. At Venlo the autobahn abruptly ended and I found myself driving on Dutch side streets. This event immediately made me think I would never get

Heidelberg Bridge

to my hotel in Leiden, a small city outside of Amsterdam. Fortunately, I was prematurely pessimistic and soon found the A-67 autobahn which headed East toward Eindhoven, The Netherlands or Eindhoven, Holland, where Dutch people live. Then I wondered, "Why aren't these natives of this beautiful country called Netherlanders?" Or, they could be called Hollandites. Again I wondered, "Where did they get the name Dutch from?" If my high school history teacher, Mr. Prehn was around I know he would surely have a logical explanation for this. Life seemed so much simpler when I was in high school.

According to my map I was to continue to the intersection of A-1 and A-67 at a spot North of Antwerp, which is in yet another country. Belgium. There I would take the A-1 North to Leiden. Sounds easy right? Wrong! I ended up following the autobahn which led me South into the heart of Antwerp. This was not what I wanted to do because Amsterdam was North of me, in the opposite direction. My inner cranial compass, the one I was born with, like a homing pigeon told me I was going South. More wet armpits! In addition, the perspiration was beading up on my forehead and continuing all the way to the back of my neck. One of the highway signs offered an option to veer off the route I was on and follow, what was called, "Ring Antwerp." I hoped this was an indication that the road would be like the three digit interstates in the United States and travel around the outskirts of Antwerp and lead me to A-1 Northbound. As soon as I came to an option that offered Amsterdam although it was not A-1, I followed it anyway. It took me through Rotterdam, a beautiful city in Holland noted for its windmills and acres of colorful tulips. Unfortunately, I never saw any of those treasures because the route I was on only displayed dark smokestacks and factories.

I then drove through Delft which was built a millennium ago and had to be rebuilt in the 1600s because its arsenal blew up and destroyed the original city. After Delft I reached Den Haag, known to me in English as The Hague. It is presently in the news because it is the location of the war crime trials of Serbian army officers accused of brutalities on Kosovo civilians. I was feeling confident now because Leiden was an option on the exit sign and I felt I was close to my destination. Home free, right? Wrong again! I exited to see the very inviting signs directing me to the Holiday Inn, which really made me feel good because I desperately had to go to the bathroom.

Through the evening rush hour traffic of Leiden, I attempted to follow those elusive Holiday Inn logos. My attempts were unsuccessful. My armpits were quite wet now. I was hopelessly lost in a maze of small Dutch towns, back streets and cobblestone paths that appeared to be used only by bicyclists. I soon got the idea from their dirty looks and comments, which I did not understand; they did not wish to share these narrow paths with my Mercedes rental. I think Hans Brinker once walked those ancient, constricted, cobblestone streets.

After several stops and inquiries and new directions to follow, some of which were in opposition to one another, I finally got the correct direction to the Holiday Inn. Unfortunately, due to road construction, I could not get in to the entrance and had to go around the city again. This was not an easy task because I was driving for nine harrowing hours, I was tired and by now I really, really had to go to the bathroom.

All was forgiven, though when I met Anke, the statuesque Dutch woman working at the registration desk. She was beautiful, she was genuinely caring, for I told her of my plight, and she was so very friendly. I was soon to find out that all Dutch women were like this. I immediately fell in love with her. I had hoped she would be like the young blonde South African girl working the registration desk at my Heidelberg Hotel. When she heard I was from New York, she asked it she could come home with me. No such luck! Anke didn't ask to come home with me. She didn't even come to my room as I had fantasized. Isn't it always that way? Fantasies never come true. Why couldn't I run across another Starmiss? Damn!

In downtown Amsterdam though, there were friendly women that would have come back with me to New York, for sure. These were really friendly women.

At that time, there were six females in my life. They were my mother, my four daughters, and Ava Brown, my Rottweiller. I am equally sure my mother and four daughters would not approve of these women with much makeup and few clothes. Ava would not mind, of this I am sure.

These overly friendly women here in Amsterdam, were not at all like Anke in Leiden who was cultured, caring and so well mannered. I mean they were friendly and all, but I don't think they were sincerely interested in anything about me except what was in my pants. I refer specifically to my wallet. These women, of the world's oldest profession worked in Amsterdam and it seemed they only wore lingerie. They sat in storefront windows in their underwear and, on close inspection, didn't seem cold. I first thought they were modeling the lingerie they were wearing but then realized they were too fat to be models. Except for one who was real skinny and had short blonde hair. She bounced up and down a lot and convulsed like Joe Cocker. I thought she was keeping time to really fast music, only there was no music. I later realized she was sort of nervous and probably took a medication that kept her so skinny. I read that methamphetamine makes people act like that.

No, I was not at all interested in taking any of these window-posing women home to NY. Mayor Guiliani, along with the five women in my life, would never approve. This was the red-light district of Amsterdam where prostitution is legal. These ladies were not at all like Anke and the other women I met in Holland, all of which were refined and classy. None of them came to my room, like in the James Bond movies, either. Damn, didn't they know I was from a secret intelligence agency?

Reality brings me back on the United States I-80 approaching Chicago and the motorcycles coming from the Sturgis rally are more numerous now. They are all big Harleys. The motorcycles on the European autobahns were mostly BMWs with the riders wearing rain gear. These were one piece suits with huge zippers that went from the chin to the crotch. They are practical but not cool looking like the American Hog bikers. I don't suppose there was any of this European apparel at Sturgis. The riders I see passing me now are wearing jeans, boots and black leather vests over their tee shirts. It is beginning to rain now and the riders are wet. Again, I feel sorry for them as I set the windshield wiper of my Lincoln to low speed and listen to Elvis singing *Heartbreak Hotel*.

CHAPTER 8

In the Beginning

It was the summer of 1978, the first adventure Alex and I had out West together. The skies were the deepest blue we had ever seen. The air was the clearest and driest we ever breathed and we never saw rain. Never, no rain, not the entire summer. The temperature rose to the 90s during the day and dropped to the 40s at night. We were never hot, nor did we ever feel cold. The weather was perfect. We spent a few weeks with the Canhams and camped at Grandby Lake. That area is remarkable by the tall, straight lodgepole pines, the only plant growth in the area. These trees are used to make telephone poles. The American Indians used them for constructing their lodges. We spent four weeks with the Canhams and enjoyed numerous excursions to Rocky Mountain beauty. We then visited Roy and Pam Howard in Longmont.

❧❧❧❧

Roy was the city manager of Longmont, Colorado at the time. Longmont is located on the Front Range about

Roy Howard

10 miles north of Boulder. He and I were bunkmates during our senior phase of the USMC Platoon Leaders Class. PLC is a college program where officer candidates spent two, six-week training sessions at Quantico, Virginia. The "training" was similar to the USMC Paris Island recruit training. It is designed to develop the toughest American fighting men. Our Quantico training included the same discipline and humiliation offered at Paris Island with emphasis on leadership training. This meant that everyday a different platoon member was responsible for the administration of the platoon's daily routine. The combination of being held to higher standards than we ever were in our lives, with respect to discipline and responsibility, was quite stressful. Roy and I have developed a bond that has remained for nearly 40 years.

The Howard's have two sons close to Alex's age and our summer adventure continued with another family. Roy had a motorboat. We trailered it to Horsehead Lake and more thrilling memories were built. This time those memories were imprinted on the background of a crystal clear lake surrounded by high bluffs.

I felt very close to Roy and Stu that summer. I was still hurting from my separation with Irene and still looking for acceptance from someone close. I am an only child and I believe Roy and Stu became surrogate brothers, which I needed so much. I will be eternally grateful to them for this.

We were on a roll! The new environments, at the Howards and the Canhams, two culturally different families connected to me by different threads, provided a view of happy family life for Alex I felt I was unable to give him.

We left the Howards and their immaculate home in Longmont. We headed West again and North towards the Grand Teton National Park. In my mind we could not even come close to the thrills and adventures we had experienced on this vacation so far. I was wrong! We would become part of an adventure that would involve us in Alex becoming a candidate for the Guinness Book of World Records.

ᴊᴊᴊ

Paul Driscoll was a friend I made during the summer of 1958. He was a lifeguard at Marine Park Beach at Great Kills. He was one of a group of Staten Island friends whose connection would last a lifetime. In the summer of 1958, I had been living on Staten Island for less than a year. I was on the cusp of severing my ties to my Brooklyn adolescent friends and building a new group of friends as I entered adulthood. At the beach in Great Kills Park, Lance

Armstrong was the lieutenant and Bill Jenson was the chief of lifeguards. Bill's father was Chuck Jenson who, 15 years later would, retire from the NY Fire Department and relocate to Salida, Colorado.

Father and Son Jensen

Bill Jensen was a true leader. He was a swimming star at Curtis High School and became a NYC lifeguard as soon as he was of age. As Chief of Lifeguards, Bill was responsible for maintaining safety on his beach and conducting the training regimen for his staff. He did so with competent professionalism. He led a four-mile run in the sand to Crookes Point every morning as an eye opener for his staff. That would be followed by the daily swim workout. Bill was all business in his orange nylon swim trunks, tan skin and aviator sunglasses. The only other adornment on his body was a pair of Zeiss binoculars given to him by his father. In order to protect the beachgoers he would often be seen using his optics searching the horizon. He was on lookout for hungry and vicious sharks that would prowl the east coast on occasion. The last known attack was in Matawan, N.J. in 1916, some 40 years earlier but Bill was always alert.

It was on this same beach that Bill met Nancy Hammel, a pretty blond Wagner College coed. They were soon to be married and currently are about to celebrate their 50th wedding anniversary.

Jim Albus, also a lifeguard, was then a great athlete at New Dorp High School. In 1958 he had just become the recipient of Staten Island's prestigious Jacques award. This award is given each year to a high school athlete considered the best on the Island. There is a committee that spends many hours in meetings deciding on the winner. It was not too difficult a choice the year that Jim won because his statistics in basketball and baseball were outstanding. Jim is now a successful golf pro on the senior tour. He was also a friend and a lifeguard at Great Kills Beach in 1958. He now resides in Sarasota, Florida with his wife Brenda who is distinguished by her grace and beauty. My daughters Nancy and Eva used to babysit for their children when they were our New Dorp neighbors.

There was a prank in the showers that was done to unsuspecting lifeguards at the end of the day. The water temperature in those showers was always a bit cool. For some reason the unsuspecting victim would feel a warm stream running down his leg. At the same time the waste water flowing down the drain would have a yellow streak in it. No one knows who the culprit was but it seems that Jim was always close by when this occurred.

It was that summer, on that beach, where we all socialized. We dug clams from the sand bars and steamed them at night over driftwood fires and washed them down with beer. It was there, on that dusty brown sand beach, that I met Irene Carroll. She was Lance's girlfriend, Carol Kubera's best friend. After one look at Irene, I immediately made it my business to become Lance's friend in order to meet and get close to this college beauty. It did not take long. I sat there at Irene and Carol's blanket with Lance, and the connection was made. I asked Irene out right on the spot. It was love at first sight. The thunderbolt had struck me. Irene and Carol were sophomores at Wagner College and had been neighbors and friends since attending their elementary school, St. Claire's RC Church in Great Kills, Staten Island.

That night I took Irene to the open air drive-in movie in Perth Amboy, New Jersey. That property became a multiplex of about 15 theaters with armed private police patrolling the lobby. There was no need for armed guards in movie theaters in 1958. The movie was *Marjorie Morningstar,* with Gene Kelly and Natalie Wood. It was a love story set during a summer camp in the Catskill Mountains. Now it was love for me which was set on a beach two miles from my home. We spent the rest of the summer double dating with Lance and Carol. In a few years, we were all married. Lance was my best man when Irene and I were married. He gave us a warm toast. A quarter a century later we were all divorced. I still consider Lance my best friend. He is a lawyer specializing in Elder Law. In those carefree days of the Eisenhower presidential administration, when we drank beer until we vomited and then laughed about it, we didn't give much thought about wills and estate planning.

Getting back to Paul Driscoll, one of the lifeguards on the beach that summer he had graduated at the top of his class from St. Bonaventure College and Notre Dame Law School. He was probably the brightest of us all, a true intellectual. His father was the principal of Tottenville High School where Irene and Carol had graduated. Upon graduation from law school, Paul was recruited by the new Kennedy presidential administration. He worked for JFK in the White House until the assassination of the youngest and America's first Catholic president. At that time Robert Kennedy, the president's brother, who was the United States Attorney General, recruited Paul Driscoll to work in the Justice Department. Paul did so for a few years until Sirhan Sirhan ended Bobby's tenure via assassination. Paul then went to work for Caesar Chavez and the Farm Workers Union on the West coast. Paul's political motivation was left of center and he worked for little pay. After seven years, Paul, for some reason, suffered legal burnout, left the law profession and the Farm Workers Union and relocated in Jackson, Wyoming. He worked as a ski patrol member, as a mountain climbing instructor, a ski instructor, and a ski apparel salesman. He was doing work and living the lifestyle he loved. When his parents died, he received an inheritance. He invested in property and built two homes, one in Jackson, Wyoming and one in Victor, Idaho. Paul also was a pioneer in white water kayaking. He explored rivers that had never been kayaked before. He was fearless as he conquered virgin waterways. There is a stretch of the Teton River in Idaho, named Driscoll's Drop, after him.

Alex and I visited Paul at his log home in Jackson. The furniture and decorations were rustic. They were made of split aspen and stole my heart. The interior log walls were adorned with the tools and toys of Paul's new trade. There were cross country skis, downhill skis, snowshoes, kayak paddles and various ski poles hung in prominent positions. He also had several beautifully framed outdoor prints and an Indian rug displayed. I felt the decor belonged in a magazine for millions to appreciate. He no longer practiced law and told me he did not miss it.

I explained to Paul that Alex and I were on a quest for adventure and wondered what he recommended for us. He thought for a moment with his jutting chin resting in his hand and then, wide-eyed, pointing a finger in the air, was struck with the itinerary. He indicated we should camp at Jenny Lake in the national park and hike to the Alaskan Basin which is located 12 miles West of the lake. We would have to climb to the Cascade Canyon Trail make an eight-mile Westward trek, climb to Hurricane Pass and then continue over the pass and then descend into the basin. He said it was a formidable and worthwhile hike. I would soon learn the meaning of Paul's word, "formidable."

꜀꜀꜀

It didn't sound too difficult, and I thought we would carry all we needed in my huge backpack. Alex had a small pack that contained his sleeping bag and light foam roll. If the going got too rough, we could always stop where we were, spend the night, and then head back the next day. The good part about a hike that challenges you with constant climbing on the way in is that the return trip is all downhill. Therefore if the weather is bad or an emergency return is necessary, it is easier coming back than it was getting there.

We began at dawn, got the required permit at the

ranger station and began our trek. We had to notify the rangers of our intentions, when we were leaving, where we were going, and when we were returning. If we didn't check back in when we were supposed to, a search would be initiated. There was no fooling around here. This was the big time and danger lurked behind every cloud in the form of surprise snow or lightening storms. There were also dangers behind trees in the form of grizzly bears and moose which must be given a wide berth. We soon realized we were not on Staten Island anymore.

Our day began with a series of switchbacks that took us up to Inspiration Point at an altitude of 7,200 feet which was about 800 feet above the smooth mirror-like lake. The view was magnificent. We were able to look down on the lake where the boat used to ferry people across appeared insect-sized. We were facing a rising sun still low over the horizon which cast a surreal beauty on the scene. We had to pass Hidden Falls, which is a thundering cascade of melting glacial waters dropping thousands of feet. The crashing water came from melting snows high on Mt. St. John and seemed to explode on the valley floor on its way to fill Jenny Lake. The sensation, smells and sounds were awesome. The pleasant smell of the sun in the dry air baking the oils of my skin offered a dimension that is hard to put into words.

After the assent up the switchbacks we then turned our backs on the huge lake and headed West along the Cascade Canyon trail. We continued on a picturesque route for a straight and level four miles. On our left and right sides were steeply rising mountains that rose more than a mile above us. Also on our left, on the valley floor was Cascade Creek, which was the recipient of numerous huge waterfalls, the product of melting ice from the Teton Glacier. The icy waters cut their way down Teewanot Mountain and Mount Owen, filling Cascade Creek with its clear liquid. We passed several moose lounging in Cascade Creek. Another element that we found to be a pleasant surprise was the numerous shrill whistles. They came from Yellow-bellied Marmots who seemed to herald our approach. They were about the size and appearance of the woodchucks of the east.

Several movies were shot in this Teton location, *Shane, Son of Lassie, Bad Bascomb, Rocky IV* and, *The Mountain Men* are some memorable films. There was never a film crew able to depict this beauty, with its sights, sounds and smells, with its awesome panorama, as it really is.

The end of Cascade Canyon was caused by the 10,000 foot Table Mountain. We followed the trail along an endless array of switchbacks that allowed us to reach higher and higher in altitude and in the sensations I was feeling within my soul. My mood was being lifted above and beyond any height it had previously achieved. We were now on the Teton Crest Trail which we would follow for eight miles to our destination, the Alaskan Basin. When we left the switchbacks of Table Mountain we were above 10,000 feet and above the tree line. Although it was August, there were patches of snow everywhere. The air temperature was about 80 degrees and our feet were trampling through corn snow. I never before had to smack a mosquito while there was snow under my feet. This was a lifetime first experience. We surely weren't on Staten Island anymore.

The trail we were following led to a sign indicating Hurricane Pass was just ahead. I was eager to set foot on Hurricane because it would be the first time I set foot on alpine tundra. Just imagine, this was the same environment as in the Arctic Circle. A problem occurred when we were met with a 30 foot high vertical wall of rock. I had not realized the pass, a series of long and gentle switchbacks, had been closed by a slide. I simply thought this was the normal way to get to the Alaskan Basin. I told Alex to give me his pack and wait below while I brought the packs to the top. All this time a huge black raven stood as lookout above us at the mouth of this closed pass. Missing a few tail feathers, which identified him as an elder of his flock, he seemed to loudly warn of our intrusion into his domain. Could he be offering a welcome? The way everything had been going so well, I know now it was a welcome. He seemed to be an appointed sentinel that guarded this narrow opening to one of nature's paradises.

After leaving our packs at the top, I climbed down and had seven-year-old Alex get in front of me and climb the vertical wall with me assisting him with encouragement and directions on what hand and foot holds to use. Inches at time and without so much as a whimper or indication of fear from my son, we got to the top. We immediately realized that the topography again had changed. It was as though we stepped out of a space ship. We were now in arctic tundra. The sparse vegetation was only about six inches high. We saw the tinniest plants with the tinniest of beautiful flowers. I will never forget a delicate yellow flower later identified as a snowlily. As we continued along this strange reddish colored landscape it seemed as though we could have been on Mars. We passed a huge red rock formation on our right that looked like a battleship. We later learned it was named Battleship Rock.

Seven Year Old Alex Crossing Hurricane Pass

There was an intense wind blowing, we were high in the atmosphere and there was no natural barrier to the weather. We were in the heavens. I stood for a moment and realized all that we had done that day, the distance we had traveled and the heights we had reached. I became swept with emotion. I felt tears on my cheeks, the warm sun on my shoulders and I experienced an incredible feeling of happiness, conquest, and invincibility. Mostly though, I felt worthiness as a parent and a person. Was this what John Denver referred to as a "Rocky Mountain High?" I was, at that point, recreated into a new identity. I no longer felt the sense of failure as a husband that I carried with me for the last two years. I was reborn, for sure. I felt an overwhelming force sweeping through me. Something big happened then in that magical setting, something spiritual, it had to be. Why were tears running down my cheeks?

We continued for the next mile and a half along the level Teton Crest Trail to the Alaskan Basin. A memorable sight in this subalpine climate was when the level trail ended and we looked down into the vast expanse of the basin. We were at 10,400 feet and were gazing at a vista some 1,100 feet beneath us. At the bottom of the bluff upon which we were standing, was a dark running animal, we first mistook for a bear but closer study identified it as a wolverine. We trekked Westward, down the switchbacks passed Sunset Lake and set up camp in a new world.

View of Sunset Lake From Hurricane Pass

All through this rugged and strenuous hike, I never heard Alex complain. When we reached the summit of Table Top Mt. and the going was strenuous at this oxygen-lacking altitude, I was taking one huge breath per step. I asked if he wanted to stop to rest, he indicated with a shrug to go on. I soon realized I needed the rests more than he did. To this day, more than three decades later, he still doesn't complain. He is easygoing, laid back and happy in his marriage to Shalini and in his job as a computer analyst and father to the talented Zander, the fourth generation of Alexes.' I am no less proud of him today than I was that night in the Alaskan Basin. In that windblown nylon tent, at that 10,400 foot altitude, I felt pride.

Hurricane Pass

We carried freeze-dried backpacker meals. All that was needed was to add water to create a nutritious and satisfying meal. We drank water from the icy swift running streams along the way and it was delicious. When we returned the following year, there were warnings everywhere in the park not to drink the water without treating it. It seems that the intestinal parasite Guardia became a threat in just one year. The lifecycle of this microbe is initiated by birds and animals defecating on the melting snows and thus they are transported to the streams, rivers, and lakes. We drank the water the previous year and that year too, thankfully we were not affected by Guardia.

Our return the next day was memorable because we marched proudly down the mountains, down the switchbacks, and down the trails, with a feeling of great conquest. Caesar's armies after conquering segments of the world could not have returned to Rome feeling any prouder than we were.

On the Cascade Canyon Trail

When we got to the ranger's shack at the end of that march, under a deep blue sky with a bright sun and virtually no humidity, we stood taller than normal as we proudly declared our safe return. The ranger didn't see the slightly built blond-haired seven-year-old Alex when we left the previous day. He looked at him now and asked if he was the Alex Flint on the permit. As he asked me, his eyes wide with amazement, never left my son. I answered that he was and asked if there was a problem. He responded by saying the pass was closed and a technical climb was necessary to get into the Alaskan Basin. I told him we climbed with no equipment and used only our bare hands and sneaker covered feet. He swiftly moved to the phone and told someone on the other end that a young boy just returned from the basin. With the phone to his ear, the ranger asked if I had any photos to prove I was there. I nodded in the affirmative showing him my Pentax .35mm SLR camera.

That was when I realized the magnitude of what we had done. This was the first time a seven-year-old boy had done what previously only technical climbers would do. Even I was not a technical climber, meaning I had no equipment, no ice ax, no carabineers, no climbing rope, etc. That was also when I had realized the danger I had subjected my only son to. The ranger indicated I should mail the photos and documents to support my claim of such a feat for a young boy to the Guinness Book of World Records people in England.

What a surprise this was! It was also a shock. Fame for my son? Elation! How incredible could a summer trip be? I was swollen with pride.

I did contact the Guinness people when we returned to Staten Island and eight months later they replied that they were refusing to open a new category for their world records. They felt that it would be too dangerous to start a category based on the youthful age of a participant in a dangerous mountain climbing event. I could see their reasoning. It could lead to child abuse by forcing children to go beyond what they were capable of. It didn't matter to me though we had participated in a once-in-a-lifetime adventure. We conquered many things the summer of '78; they changed us forever.

୬୬୬

Several years later on December 2, 1985, I was saddened by the news that Paul Driscoll died. On the front page of the *Staten Island Advance* there was a story report-ing Paul's death. The report indicated that he was killed in an avalanche, as a member of the ski patrol. He was setting dynamite charges so the falling snow banks would not be a danger to skiers. When I told the now 14-year-old Alex, he reminded me of a conversation with Paul I had forgotten. Paul told us of how they would set the charges and then ski down the mountain in front of the thundering white death. The rush he said was awesome. He explained it was like surfing in front of the killer monster waves on Hawaii's North shore.

Now Paul is gone too.

Staten Island Advance
Ex-Islander killed in Wyo. Avalanche
Staten Island Advance
December 8, 1985
By Jim Hughes
Advance Staff Writer

A former Staten Island man was killed in a Wyoming ava-lanche Monday when a column of snow five-feet deep and 100-feet wide buried him while he was on ski patrol.

Paul Driscoll, 48, who was born in Grasmere and lived in Concord until 1960, was working with five other ski pa-trollers at the Jackson Hole Ski Area when the avalanche began, around 4 p.m., according to Sheriff Roger Millward of the Jackson Hole police.

Millward said Driscoll and the other patrollers had been putting up signs for the new ski season. "He was farthest down the mountain, so he got the brunt of it," the sheriff said. "He was buried under about six feet of snow." A second patroller was also killed.

Millward said earlier in the day the patrollers had used explosives to test the snow banks to make sure they were safe. The sheriff speculated that because 'conditions changed," or perhaps because other skiers were in the area, the snow gave way.

"We have a number of deaths due to skiing, but that was the first actual fatality of a patrolman in the ski area," he said.

Millward said Driscoll had worked as a patrolman at the ski resort for four years, but had been skiing in the area for 15 years.

Driscoll was a graduate of Curtis High School, St. Bonaventure University and Notre Dame Law School. He served in the Army as a lieutenant in the ROTC program from 1958 to 1960, and was stationed in Fort Knox, KY.

From 1964 to 1966 he worked as a lawyer for the Legal Aid Society in Washington. He worked for the same organization in California from 1966 to 1971. He then moved to Jackson Hole, practiced law before turning to skiing as a profession.

He also enjoyed hiking, jogging and white water rafting.

Driscoll is survived by two sisters, Maryanne Gomme and Sister Martha Driscoll.

Funeral arrangements are being handled by the Valley Mortuary in Jackson Hole, with cremation at the Chapel of Flowers, Ogden, Utah. There will be a memorial service tomorrow at 3:30 p.m. at the foot of the mountain where Driscoll was killed. On Staten Island, a memorial Mass will be held Dec. 15 at 2 p.m. in St. Sylvester's R.C. Church, Concord.

CHAPTER 9

Marital Madness

I passed the horror of Chicago traffic and was now on the Indiana Turnpike heading East. The urban, poorly marked expressway that passes just South of Chicago and through Gary, Indiana always prevents a relaxing ride. When truck traffic is heavy and traffic is slow, which was every time I rode through there, it is difficult to see the overhead exit signs because the huge 18 wheelers block out the view. I am the driver, on this nerve-wracking stretch of road sitting ramrod straight in the seat and can be distinguished by his blue knuckles, which is an anomaly that occurs from squeezing the juice out of my leather covered steering wheel. I always have wet armpits on this stretch of highway.

When I get to Indiana and its clean, relaxing turnpike, I always hit the first rest stop to gas up and get a cup of coffee. I usually follow the same routine when heading West in anticipation of the Chicago horror. One year on the way West I met a strikingly attractive middle-aged woman at the rest stop who asked if she could share a table with us at the fast-food greaser. She sat with me and Alex with her interesting personality as she proceeded to tell us of her life's troubles. Her name was Jane. She was once from NY and was presently leaving Florida looking to relocate in California.

It seems Jane's ex-husband, a former NYC Policeman, had a secret girl-friend while they were still living in NY. Jane's parents had retired to the East coast of Florida several years earlier and left Jane and her husband and their sons the house in Queens, NY. When Jane's husband indicated he had a teaching job on the West coast of Florida, Jane's parents signed the house over to their daughter and it was sold. A new house was purchased in Florida under names of both Jane and husband, who still had the same girlfriend on the side. Florida is a community property state so all that was left to Jane by her parents was now half owned by her husband. I'll bet you can guess the rest of the story.

Bozo, that is what I will call the husband, immediately sued for divorce, which he was granted. He then told his wife the new house in Florida had to be sold so he could get his share. Sounded like extortion to me, which I thought was a crime. I was wrong. Jane had to get financial help from her family to pay off Bozo so he would go away and leave his trail of misery and destruction behind. The destruction was in the form of three adolescent sons left in complete confusion. He did go away, but not very far because he did have a job in the community. His girlfriend soon became his wife and life went on. Jane's parents, remember them? They were hurt too. They were the ones who gave the NY house to their loving daughter and her, Bozo husband. They also relocated to the West coast of

Florida in anticipation of a happily ever after. These generous people were proud to take up residence near their married daughter and her family, but in doing so left their social circle on the Florida East coast. It was an emotionally devastating act that Bozo committed.

Jane was a cancer survivor. One son joined a religious commune and has not been heard from in 10 years, she said sadly. A second son has a criminal record, something to do with attacking policemen whenever he is drunk. The third son is devoted to his mother but suffers from guilt because he has his own family to care for in upstate NY. Jane's elderly parents fared even worse. Her father soon died because he had such difficulty dealing with his wife who began to suffer depression. Mother was placed in a home where she, heavily medicated, tells the sad story to all who will listen.

Bozo did not get off as easy as Jane. He is despised by Jane's family and his sons. The girlfriend he married and set up house with had been widowed twice before. Husband number one had a heart attack he did not survive. Husband number two, it turned out was a former coworker of Bozo, a NY City cop, ate his gun. That is, he placed a .38 Special against the roof his mouth and squeezed the trigger. Bozo, who was the picture of athletic health before he met the two-time widow, had to undergo a quadruple bypass within three years of his sad marriage. It seems the multi-widow, who looked like a blonde cross between a Playboy Bunny and an Amsterdam hooker enjoyed promiscuous behavior whenever her husband was not around. In addition to public humiliation, she seemed to enjoy sexually humiliating her husbands privately. I wonder if she would she be called a black widow or a pink widow?

After his heart surgery, Bozo told ex-wife Jane, that his present wife continually belittled his manhood size and his lovemaking techniques. Bozo actually came to Jane for comforting. Thankfully, it wasn't given. He indicated to Jane that none of this happened until they were married. It seems that size of his external organ that was ample enough to satisfy Blonde before the wedding instantly became inadequate after they were married. This son of a bitch wanted his ex-wife to take him back. Imagine telling this to an ex-wife he had cheated on? Jane had none, nor did she show any sympathy. As I listened with great interest to this story, I thought to myself, "Sometimes there is justice in this world."

Jane heard an abbreviated account of my marital story and told me she was touched by my devotion to my children. She asked for my address, which I gave her and she sends me a Christmas card every year from San Dimas, CA. She is remarried to a dentist and is happy with her life. Bozo is divorced from Blonde and in poor health. Although he asks, Jane will not take him back. Not ever.

This story all transpired at a rest stop, over a cheeseburger, fries and a coke. I could never forget it. It impressed me with a behavioral pattern identified with narcissism. Somehow Bozo was never taught the meaning of unselfishness.

CHAPTER **10**

Closet Elves

We were on the Ohio Turnpike approaching Toledo, an area Alex notated in his journal on our second trip in 1979. He mentioned it was an area that played good music. He would make comments that were noteworthy and end the sentence, *"It happened that way, going West."* The most memorable comment in that journal was in connection with the excitement we had on I-80 in the eastern part of Nebraska.

I remember it was a Sunday morning in July. I was driving my 1978 black Chevy van, the one Alex called it Darth Vader. It was equipped with a CB radio. Those trucker types of radios were popular in the 1970s. We were part of the heavy westbound traffic approaching Lincoln, Nebraska when a bronze sedan with two elderly riders who were part of the eastbound traffic distinguished themselves. This would have been a simple scene of mainly Sunday morning church goers except for one remarkable aspect. The bronze sedan with an elderly man driving and his female passenger, for no particular reason, initiated a leftward movement that livened up that quiet Sunday morning. They did so by traveling East in the Westbound lane. They were coming head on into traffic. I hit the brake and allowed them to pass on my right as they continued on their merry, but panicked, way. Alex was in the passenger seat of the van, which in itself, was remarkable because he usually was in the bed in the rear.

"Wow," he said.

"Shit," I answered.

"Did you see that?" As I reached up for the CB mike attached to the headliner over the rear-view mirror, keyed the button and calmly announced to a quiet channel 19, "There is an East-Bounder in the Westbound lane." The radio immediately came to life with screams of inquiry as to what our 10-20 (location) was. While watching the event, now behind me, in my side-view mirror, and looking for a mileage marker on the side of the highway, I kept somewhat abreast of the situation. I was able to see the errant vehicle, with an elderly driver and passenger, come to rest, undamaged, on the right shoulder. At the same time we passed a mileage marker and I was able to announce to the entire CB radio world the location of the near disaster.

I saw cars hitting brakes and stopping straight in their tracks, some cars turned to their right to stop, thus spinning in a clockwise direction, other cars turned left to stop and spun in a counter-clockwise direction. It was like a scene in black and white from a Laurel and Hardy movie. The Westbound traffic behind us came to a complete stop. It was as though there was a traffic light that magically appeared in Eastern Nebraska on I-80 and our black van ran through the yellow signal and the rest of the traffic obeyed the red. We continued on our way with nothing behind us and Alex reached for his journal and noted the date, time, place and circumstances. He then ended the paragraph with "*It happened that way, going West.*"

I don't know where that journal is now. I do know I never would have thrown it out. I suppose it is somewhere among my belongings hidden away in a secret location in the attic, garage, basement or the rear of an unused closet. The location is known only to my attic and closet elves. I am referring to the only living creatures who know where everything is, whether hidden or lost. Sometimes I think while rooting around looking for an item that is lost or missing that these are the magical forces responsible. Tiny, mischievous, mysterious beings who work to keep locations of needed items from being found. Perhaps if they kind, they will reveal the location of my lost and wanted things to me.

I have sensed the presence of these dudes ever since I was a child. I don't believe there is much scientific evidence to support my belief, but I remain convinced of their existence. When I was married, I always felt it was my wife who put valuables away in an irretrievable location. Now that I have been single for so many years I am certain the hiders of important things are not wives at all. They are closet elves. I am sure of that now. I know they are there because I have heard them, mostly at night, and found their droppings. I just do not know why they are so spiteful. They always seem to be around when my stress level is high. It has always been that way with me, except when I was married. During my married years I heard no closet noises, found no elf droppings, and always blamed my spouse for my missing treasures. Probably one of the main reasons men marry is to give them someone to blame. Some day there will be a study to prove this theory.

Regardless of discovering the location of that precious journal, I will write from memory. The wife or elf has not been born yet who will hide my memory from me. I expect that day will come too, but not for another 40 years I hope.

One magical day some 30 years later, I found Alex's journal. It is reprinted exactly as he wrote it in 1979 and 1981, in Chapter 14, *A Boy's Travel Journal.*

CHAPTER 11

Stuff Happens!

Someone once said that life is made up of 10% of what happens to you, and 90% of how you responded to it.

During the Christmas vacation of 1978, I was thrilled to be invited by the daughter of a close family friend to spend a few days skiing at the farmhouse she rented in Vermont. She was an attractive young woman who had recently graduated from nursing school. She had taken her first job in the beautiful New England countryside. Linda and her family knew of my recent single status and I was invited to spend a few days in her company. I was promised I would get to meet some single nurses from her hospital. At this time of my life, I was excited at the prospect of new female companions.

I drove North up Interstate 95 through a scenic winter wonderland that enhanced my mood. My shiny, topaz black, 78 Chevy conversion van stood out in stark contrast to the stunning snow-laden countryside. It created a capsule of beauty. A picture of this combination could have been a prize-winning General Motors magazine layout.

When I exited the interstate and began the drive on the quaint state roads the landscape actually improved. There were dark green fir trees mixed with the bare branches of deciduous trees, all the limbs where draped with a white fluff. I felt as though I was driving through a scene from a Currier and Ives print.

There was no GPS navigation system back then and I following the directions Linda had given me, soon found the farmhouse. Her residence completed the Christmas card painting I was enjoying. At three in the afternoon, the long December blue gray shadows created by the tree trunks and the sagging yellow sun enhanced the scene for an even greater memory. The ancient two-story white farmhouse had green shudders. It was framed by a huge barn with cupola and weather vane. The circular driveway was recently plowed and left ample room to park my black jewel.

Linda, a honey blond, was right there to greet me with an enthusiastic hug as soon as I climbed down from the van. She handed me a warm glass of glug, a heated wine with raisons and spices of which cinnamon was the most prominent. Linda helped me with my two bags and insisted that my ski boots should be the first item to be placed in the warm house. "This is so your feet don't freeze on the slopes tomorrow," she explained, "It will drop to below zero tonight." "If your boots are frozen in the morning, you will be uncomfortable all day," she explained.

I was enthused by this environment. The anticipation of finding a small dot on a map and of using the directions she gave me to successfully navigate my way here, added to my happy mood.

I entered through a mud room, an appendage Linda

explained that was built into every farmhouse, which led to the kitchen. There was an antique stove, a holdover from the 1930s. It was a wood burning affair that, along with the simmering tomato sauce, created a soothing aroma. The pleasant feeling I had at that moment was borderline euphoria. After the scenic and relaxing five-hour ride, this arrival held a promise of a pleasant stay.

Boy, was I wrong!

We sat on a comfortable sofa in the living room which was heated by a round metal wood stove that had a shiny metal chimney running up to a point near the ornate tin ceiling. The warm glug magically transformed to me to a resident of Nirvana.

Just a few minutes ago, I was in the New England countryside, on an unknown country road, and in a mild state of panic from feeling lost. I always get that way when following directions to a new location. Now, I was seated on a soft sofa with my feet stretched out on a low table, in front of a warm fire, watching a buxom, smiling young woman sorting out chopped leaves on a Frisbee.

I asked if it was oregano for the tomato sauce, whose inviting smell permeated the house. With a huge smile and flashing eyes Linda replied, "Nooo, it's not oregano, its pot." "Haven't you ever had this before" she asked with a shy look. "What is pot?" awkwardly I questioned. She discontinued her attention to the Frisbee and looked at me asking, "You mean you have never smoked marijuana before?" "No, I am a runner, I don't smoke." "It's not the same as cigarettes; those things will kill you," she countered. Linda had my attention now. I observed her intense sorting more closely. There were seeds and stems she was separating from small leaves. When she was satisfied with

the separation, she picked up a small package of rolling papers. After removing a thin sheet of paper from the
pack, she adeptly held the paper in the fingers of her left
hand. With the Frisbee balanced on her lap, she sprinkled
the flecks of leaves into the paper and tenderly cradled the
leaves in the paper. Then, using two hands, she rolled the
leaves into a tube resembling a cigarette. Looking at me,
with a slight smile that almost never left her, she held the
joint up to her mouth and with her pink, wet tongue, and
licked the flap. After forming the near perfect white cylinder, she inserted the entire joint into her mouth and, still
with her eyes on me, she sensually withdrew the moistened
cylinder through her puckered lips. She then laid it aside
and began the process again. She made six joints that way
and kept her eyes evenly divided between me and her task.
She had my total attention.

The pleasant combination of events, the scenic beauty, the trip, the farmhouse, the cooking smells, the warm
wine glug, Linda's warmth and now the inhaling of this
strange narcotic put me into a completely relaxed state.
The feeling was like nothing I had ever felt before. I liked
it. My thoughts moved ahead to the arrival of Linda's nurse
friends.

Somehow, I don't remember when the music began. It
was from the *Eagles Greatest Hits* album. I soon heard the
sounds of The Band, Fleetwood Mac, and then the music
of Meatloaf. I wondered if heaven would be like this. At
Linda's suggestion of dinner, I realized that I was incredibly
hungry. She led me by the hand to the kitchen, where the
table was set for two. A single candle in an antique brass
holder burned in the center of the table. That small flame
provided the only light in that kitchen. We ate a dinner of

homemade Italian bread, spaghetti, and tomato sauce. We drank Chianti. The combination of aromas, tastes and atmosphere was exquisite.

After eating, I must have given a sign of being tired because I was led back into the living room, given a pillow from the couch and offered a spot on the oval hooked rug in front of the fireplace. I don't know how long I slept. But I awoke with a start. It was Linda. She was kneeling next to me, one hand on my chest, the other behind my head lifting it. Her lips were against mine and she was moaning softly. I pushed away as a matter of reflex and immediately experienced a guilt-orientated mood change.

Linda's father was a lifelong family friend. He was like an older brother to me. He took me fishing and to ball games when I was a kid. I couldn't engage in what I soon realized was Linda's plan from the beginning. There were no other nurses coming that night as I had originally been told. It was just the two of us.

I don't remember what I said, but Linda replied, "My father told me I'd better behave." I guess she wasn't obeying his wishes. It didn't end there. We soon went upstairs to sleep and I realized my bed was in a cove off Linda's bedroom. There were no doors. She again made an obvious move to seduce me. This time she was wearing a nightgown, and in the dim, candle lit room of this Victorian farmhouse I could see right through it.

Thinking about this incident now, I don't know how I said, "Your father is like my brother, and I couldn't do this to him." If she persisted though, I believe I would have succumbed to nature. If there was just one more attempt by her to pursue what she obviously planned for a long time, I am sure I would have given in. To this day, I don't know how I resisted although I am glad though that I did. Had I entered her antique brass double bed that night, I would have suffered guilt. The guilt would have been a burden I did not need.

When I awoke the next morning, in that bucolic Vermont farmhouse, Linda had prepared a large breakfast. There was fresh-squeezed orange juice, farm eggs, bacon, home-made bread, local blueberry jelly and rich dark coffee.

Again the combination of aromas in that quaint structure, which seemed to absorb the morning sunshine, was awesome. There was the excitement we shared of the promise of beautiful day with weather to match on Killington's ski slopes. We skied down the mountain, we laughed as we fell, and we spent enjoyable moments as we rode the lift to the top of the mountain. The surrounding ice crystals that bathed the tree tops around us created a magical scene.

We had a sandwich for lunch at the restaurant and I announced that I had to go. It was then that I noticed a wave of failure in Linda's face. It was the first time I saw her without a smile.

On the ride back to NY, I thought her disappointment was due to me leaving early. Not for many months later did I realize how deep her despair must have been. Linda wanted me as a father for her beautiful, yet unborn baby.

❧❧❧

When I returned to Staten Island I called my friend, Steve Kelly. I had coached Steve in gymnastics and rode motorcycles with him. That following spring would have him coach me in the ways of rodeo riding. Steve was part of a large network of friends I got to hang out with. He had told me they had planned a New Year's Eve Party at a Ramada Inn located off Interstate 80 in Newark, New Jersey. I was happy to attend. This was only three days after the incident with a close family friend's daughter where I resisted being seduced. I was still emotionally shaken by the almost affair and didn't realize it.

At that Ramada party I drank more Tequila than they have in Tijuana. Now, whenever I get together with the Kelly family I am reminded of that event. There are photos of me filling green derby party hats. I was filling the hats with a green substance emerging from my innards. The more I vomited, the more hats I was handed, and the more hats I filled, the more I vomited. I spent the entire New Years Day in a bed in someone's room. The television was on and in a dazed sleep, I heard snippets of football games begin and end. I also vaguely remember the other bed being used by a couple engaged in lovemaking. In the dense, sad, sick haze I was in, I heard a girl say, "What about him?" The response was, "Don't worry, he is out of it."

More than 30 New Year's Eves have passed since that cold Vermont night. I allowed the emotional trauma of rejecting Linda's advances to evident itself that New Year's Eve, by drinking in such excess. I often wonder how much more alcohol I would have needed if I had allowed myself to succumb to that well-planned seduction.

CHAPTER 12

Family Ties

When I was in Hollywood, Florida to celebrate the new millennium with my parents, I asked my mother about our Sicilian ancestry. The tale she related was quite convoluted and I did my best to organize it into an understandable story.

My mother's maiden name is Livoti. Her father's name was Carmelo Livoti, born in 1877, and his father was Filippo Neri Livoti, born in 1835.

Filippo Neri was born with the last name of Simone. Mom did not know her great-grandfather's first name but through the diligent research of cousin, Joe Livoti, it was found to be Giovanni Simone.

I did hear an interesting story to explain the origin of the Livoti name. It seems that Mom's great grandfather, Giovanni Simone murdered a man who paid romantic attention to his widowed mother. He committed this act of justice when he was a teenager. According to the culture of that beautiful island, it was expected of Sicilian males to care for and protect their mothers. After shooting the hapless man, who must have been either the village idiot or from another country because he obviously didn't know of the code, Great-Grandfather Filippo Neri fled to a village on the other side of the mountain. He lived there with relatives and used the last name Livoti, his mother's maiden name. Making that village of Mazzara San Andrea his home, he married Carmela Pietrafitta, born in 1841. They had eight children together. They were named Giovanni, 1862; Concetta, 1865; Tommaso, 1867; Giuseppe, 1870; Orazio, 1873; Carmelo, 1877; Rosalia, 1881; and Candida, 1884.

In Sicily, if you come from the mountains you are referred to as a goat. If you come from the lowlands you are referred to as a frog. Frogs and goats were always wary of each other and it was taught by both groups to treat each other with suspicion. My family came from a long line of goats and to this day I would much rather be in the mountains rather than swamps.

My great grandfather, Filippo Neri made his new home in Mazzara San Andrea which is a short donkey ride of eight kilometers down the mountain to Furnari and another four kilometers to Falcone. Falcone is the home of many frogs. In one sense the frogs here were lucky because they were located on the shore of the Tirreno Sea which borders the north shore of Sicily. It is quite beautiful, I am told, and it was considered shameful that the frogs were located so close to such natural beauty.

After relocating to Mazzara, Great Grandfather soon married and begot five sons and three daughters. He was quick to tell the story to his sons that if he should die they must protect the honor of their mother just like he did with his mother. They must kill, and even die if necessary because protecting your mother is the most important thing in this life. His oldest son, Giovanni, remembered the story several decades later when a great crisis fell upon him. It seems that he was away to Palermo on a business trip. I am not sure what the business was, but logically, it would have been of an agricultural nature. While he was gone, a rumor was circulated regarding his wife's faithlessness. His wife's name has been forgotten over the years because she was always known by her pet name. Sicilians are known for attaching nicknames to everyone. I am not sure why, other than it being a part of the culture. She was called Bella which translated to English, means beauty.

Great-Uncle Giovanni confronted Great-Aunt Beauty with the rumored accusation. She denied it completely. Giovanni instantly thought to confront the man but realized if he did, he would surely kill him. Also he realized if he did kill him, the message would be that the rumor was true, which it was not. It was a dilemma that was able to be worked out. Giovanni, using Sicilian logic, told his wife, "To show you are innocent, you must kill the man who slandered you." For it to be more acceptable the plan was for Great-Aunt Beauty to shoot the man from their balcony. The proper message would be sent and family honor would be preserved.

Great-Aunt Bella sat on the balcony all day until the perpetrator of mean and vicious lies appeared. She picked up the short-barreled shotgun, took quick aim, and from a distance of 15 feet, shot the man dead. He didn't die quickly when he fell to the ground. He lay there with his blood mixing with the mud of the street. He was aware of the running chickens, barking dogs and braying donkeys. His last memory was of the screams of recrimination. Who could be so angry to yell, "Disgrazia, bastado and figliolo de puttana?"

Angry mothers often called their children these names when they were troublesome. The terms meant, *disgrace, bastard,* and *child of a whore.* They were pronounced *"Des grot zee ada,"* and with a bit greater enunciation came *"Bastia,"* with emphasis on the *"Ba."* Then after taking a breath and in a lower voice would always come *"Vee gue du putana."* At this word there was a dramatic spitting out of the word *butan.* The shouts were always accompanied by wild hand gestures. I remember these expressions from my earliest days. Sometimes though, I heard, "figliolo de puttana" used as a term of endearment. This was usually reserved for very cute infants. When I got older I began to wonder if the mothers who called their children these curses were also maligning their own character.

Let's get back to the man dying in the muddy street under the balcony of Great Aunt Beauty. History forgets his name. His last thoughts were probably of his wife, who was the Bella's sister-in-law. Yes, this was the husband of Great-Uncle Giovanni's sister, his cognato. My Great-Aunt Concetta was now a widow. Uncle never liked him anyway, it was said he always had a big mouth. Now the family would have to send Concetta to America to live on Elizabeth Street in New York City. She could not live with the shame of having a slandering husband's grave so near. After all, it was just a rumor that got him killed. In Sicily, it is also said that all rumors are usually true. Anyway, it was off to America for Concetta where she was to remarry a man, who may have been known as, Dedio. This too, was a nickname. For Bella, it endearingly referred to her beauty. For deprived Dedio, who was quite poor, his nickname meant, "Man of God." It is also possible the man was known as Debio, meaning, "Man of poverty." My mother's memory was sketchy on this point. Concetta lived a happy life in America. Dedio never was shot at, nor were there any rumors regarding his slandering innocent women. As far as everyone knew, Dedio was always loyal to Great-Aunt Concetta, although he always remained poor. As far as Great Uncle Giovanni and Great Aunt Bella, they remained happily married in Palermo, Sicily until the end of their days.

〰〰〰

Great-Grandfather Filippo Neri Livoti had a total of eight children. Great-Uncle Giuseppe Livoti was the most successful. He was the first in his family to arrive in America, landing in New York in 1896. He went into the chicken market business in New York and invested his profits in real estate. He was successful in his businesses and he was soon able to send for his brothers. He also sent significant financial support back to his hometown of Mazzara San Andrea. There is a monument erected in his honor in the town square. He was knighted by Vittorio Emmanuelle and given the rank of Cavaliere in 1933. Great-Uncle Giuseppe married the beautiful and educated Marie Piccolo also from Mazzara. They had two sons who died as toddlers and six daughters all of which were sent to Switzerland for their educations. Their daughter Carmela became a published poet and was my mother's Godmother. If an actress were picked to play the role of Carmela in *The Saga of Elizabeth Street*, it would have to be Isabella Rossalini because of the strong physical resemblance. His brother Tomaso, worked with him operating the chicken markets and one of them today is the only remaining chicken market in New York City. The health code of New York City now forbids chicken markets. A law was passed by the New York City Council and the Livoti Chicken Market was 'grandfathered in' and allowed to continue its operation as long as it remains a family operation.

Cavaliere Giuseppe Livoti

There was also a brother Oratzio. When I questioned this name, my mother explained its English derivative is Horatio. I remember this man when I was a child. He always had a thick handlebar mustache, and a small, strongly aromatic cigar. There was always a demi tasse cup of espresso in his hand and a fedora on his head. He used to sit on a wire back chair in front of Uncle Patsy's restaurant on Elizabeth Street.

My grandfather's name was Carmelo. He had a toothbrush mustache, a crew cut and deep blue eyes. Grandfather died 10 years before I was born and my only memory of him was from an 8 X 10 hand-colored photograph on my grandmother's dresser. As a small child, I was always frightened of that picture because the mustache made him resemble Adolf Hitler. He was in the produce business and when getting his start in this country, he sold fruits and vegetables from a push cart that he wheeled from place to place. There was no delivery service in those days. He had to wheel his empty push cart to the Washington Market on the West Side of Manhattan and then push the heavy load back to the Italian neighborhoods on the East Side of Manhattan. Eventually he got a horse and wagon to make life easier and more profitable. These profits soon allowed Grandfather to buy a truck and expand to farming. He leased farms in Cape Charles, Virginia, located on its eastern shore and in Tarboro, North Carolina. He was then able to realize greater profits because he was selling his own produce, thereby eliminating the middle man. My grandfather was loved by his neighbors on Elizabeth Street because he always gave them the produce that he didn't sell that day. When he died there were seven flower cars behind his hearse. In those days your importance and value in life was measured by the size of your funeral. In 1928, Grandfather's funeral was the largest ever seen on Elizabeth Street.

᠌᠌᠌᠌)))ᡕ

When my grandfather first came to America he settled on 111th Street and 11th Avenue. That neighborhood is now referred to as Spanish Harlem. It was there that he was victimized by the Black Hand. They were a loosely organized gang that preceded the Mafia. They wanted him to pay for the right to do business in this country. He refused and his pushcart was burned.

When his ship delivered him into this country in 1904, as he passed the Statue of Liberty, which was a symbol of hope to so many. He never thought he would have to endure violent bully tactics such as this. He arose before dawn every morning and worked hard for his money. Grandfather used his brawn to muscle a heavy wooden pushcart with huge spokes on the metal rimmed wheels. He endured the misery of being outdoors in all forms of unpleasant weather. In particular he hated the cold. He remembered the day he was so cold his teeth actually suffered pain. No! He would not share his profits with such bastardo. He would move away and start over someplace else. The decision he made was to move to Elizabeth Street which is located downtown, on the East Side of NY. It was where his brother Guiseppe was located with his successful chicken market. He had advised him to move there. Grandfather's main concern was to be free from the harassment of the disgrazia extortionists.

Giuseppe was right, this new location was ideal. He planned to marry and raise a family. On Elizabeth Street there was PS 25, a nearby elementary school that his children could attend. It was located across the street from his tenement. Our Lady of Loretto RC church where they could worship was also located on the same street. Grandfather could pick up his produce at the Washington Market to the West and he could set up his cart and sell to the heavily populated Jewish neighborhood just a few blocks to the East. Angela would be happy to shop on Orchard Street where, to this day, great clothing bargains could be found. The down side was that the Bowery was located one block to the East. It was a street riddled with bars, drunks, and transient bums. He would tell his family to avoid that area. They would listen to him. He was the head of his family and they were Sicilians.

Family of Carmelo and Angela Livoti
Joe 'Minx,' Candida 'Kay,' Phillip,
Grandmother Angela, Grandfather Carmelo,
John, Rose, Carmella 'Millie,' Connie, Grace

My grandfather knew the neighborhood was a good one. He knew that it was a safe place to raise his children. He had five daughters and realized the importance of a street where his children would be watched over by his neighbors while they played in front of their homes. They were the original neighborhood watch.

I was once told a story that emphasized this very point. In the early 1920s, a teen age girl from the block between Spring Street and Prince Street was returning home from work one evening. She worked in the Puch Building located on Houston Street and West Broadway. A man had fondled her as she left the building. She broke free from him and hurried in an easterly direction along Houston Street. The man, about 40 years of age, with balding brown hair and a ruddy complexion, followed her. The young girl was running as she made the turn onto Elizabeth Street from Houston Street. She saw several familiar young men in front of a restaurant and tearfully told them a man had groped her. She was terrified as she told them he was following her home. Filippo told her, "Stop running and walk to your house." The men immediately felt a duty to protect this frightened neighborhood girl. Then, almost immediately, a stranger turned the corner and observed the street until he spotted the girl walking toward Prince Street. The bald man quickened his pace and headed in her direction. The three men standing near the corner of Houston Street immediately took note of this and acted as though they were disinterested. When the stranger was a half block away they followed him to the door of the young girl's tenement. A woman across the street noticed the girl, who she knew since birth, enter her house. A few moments later she saw a strange man follow her in. She was alert to this unusual occurrence but then saw three young men, who she also knew from the neighborhood, enter behind the stranger. The woman then heard shouting from inside the hallway of the building. She soon heard a commotion on the roof. Among the words she clearly understood were "desgrazia," " bastardo," and "figliolo de puttana." She looked up in time to see the bloodied man sailing downward to the hard pavement of Elizabeth Street. He landed with a thump. It was a very loud thump.

When the police arrived the street was empty. Also absent was the usual sight of women sitting with their elbows on the window sills. Everyone questioned acted completely surprised with no idea about what had happened. There were whispers though among the neighbors. The close-knit neighborhood of Elizabeth, Mulberry and Mott Streets relayed in hushed tones that the three young men were Mario, Cheech, and Fully. This rumor never reached the ears of the police and the residents, shrugging their shoulders, never let on why that broken, beaten, bloody, body was lying in the street. The police investigation uncovered the fact that the deceased had been previously arrested for sexual misconduct, criminal trespass, and rape. Despite the evidence of spit on the face of the deceased, the event was reported that a trespasser had fallen to an accidental death.

Carmelo was beginning to enjoy a greater prosperity than ever existed in Harlem. A voice inside told him this peaceful existence would have to end. When that happened, he would deal with it. Didn't his ancestors always have to deal with adversity? Wasn't his homeland conquered so many times by the barbarians? Those, "bastardo, ah disgrazia." Those, "figliolo de puttana." As his ancestors confronted their problems in the past he would deal with his. He knew his home would always be protected. His shotgun was always in the corner of his bedroom. It was loaded and the hammers were always cocked. He would be ready.

ↄↄↄↄ

The dreaded day came. He was told he needed to pay protection if he wanted to remain in business. Carmelo didn't know what to do. He would pay protection in Harlem and he would not pay it here. While tearfully relating this event to his wife Angela, he was overheard by his son, my Uncle Filippo. Uncle Phil, as he came to be known to me in the next generation, was an adolescent who never went to school. He disliked the nuns and would rather work with his father. Besides, he couldn't submit to the restrictions that were brought on by an institutional environment. He was also known for never ever being pushed around, not in school and not in the street. Some people referred to him as Philly Pazzo, meaning Crazy Philly. He was never called this to his face, of this I am sure. You have to have known him to understand why. Uncle Phil was short in stature with straight, jet black hair and the light blue eyes of his mother. What he lacked in height he made up for in spunk. He never backed down from an argument or a fight. When he was disrespected he would pick the time and place and like a viper, promptly strike back.

I can only imagine the emotions that swept over my youthful uncle at that time. I don't think he considered many options. The police were not to be trusted at the

Uncle Phillip Livoti, 1940

time and the Sicilian code dictated that you never go to the police. Firstly, they were all Irish. Secondly, they were probably being paid off by the extortion gang. The police were not an option. My uncle responded with the only course of action his Sicilian heritage and family history dictated. He took the family gun, a 28-gauge side-by-side shotgun, it was already loaded with two shells. All Italian families had guns, and he sat on the steps of the bully who demanded extortion from his father. When the criminal returned home, there were echoes of gunshots in the night. My uncle just wanted to talk to the man. He wanted to ask him why his father had to pay protection. He wanted to reason with the man. As the extortionist approached and Filippo saw the sneer on the lips of the feared neighborhood thug, Uncle knew there would be no conversation. He pointed the weapon at the doomed bully's chest and fired twice. The tenement dwellers knew enough not to open their doors or look out their windows when Sicilian justice was being enacted. This behavior made it easier to swear ignorance, with innocent faces, to the Irish investigating officers that would soon question them. Children were taught at an early age, "Non Capito Niente," *Don't say anything.* As the bully lay bleeding to death and Uncle Phil ran away there were no windows or doors opened to observe the event. It was no secret as to who omicida *murdered* the bastardo. No one ever mentioned it to my grandfather. No police came to 238 Elizabeth Street that night or the next day. No one ever said a thing to my Uncle Phil. Everyone just knew.

Uncle Philly, which was for some reason always pronounced, "Fully," did not go through his life without amassing enemies. He was 'hit' on three separate occasions. He always survived the assassination attempts, healed from his wounds, and then settled the score in his favor.

On one occasion, while crossing the Bowery, he was hit by car and knocked to the ground. The driver then ran over my uncle, stopped the car, backed over his body and then shifted into low gear and drove away again passing over him for a total of three times. Witnesses thought Uncle Phil was dead. Weren't they surprised when he began to moan. When he raised his head to look around him all the witnesses disappeared fearing they would run afoul of the perpetrators. I was told that my uncle crawled home to his apartment at 238 Elizabeth Street. He lay on a bed in the same room that he was born in. He lay there for several weeks until he healed. I was never given the specifics of how he settled the score with his tormentors. As expected, Uncle Phil maintained his reputation and Mr. Provenzano, the local funeral director, had new clients.

A day or so after December 12, 1938, when I was born, family and friends visited my mother at the Parkway Hospital on the maternity floor and on the same day visited Uncle Phil on a different floor. In one room of that hospital I was being welcomed into the world and in another room "Fully" was being bid goodbye. He was recovering from a kidney removal that was damaged by trauma from a .38 caliber slug. No one thought he would survive. He did. He enacted his vengeance, and he survived for another 44 tumultuous years.

꙳꙳꙳

When Mario Puzo wrote *The Godfather*, it was said that none of the characters were based on real people. What he did was to create characters based on composites from many individuals. The assassin character, Luca Brazzi, bears a strong resemblance to Uncle Phil's exploits. The Robert Deniro character of a young Vito Corleone when he kills the extortionist during the San Gennaro Feast is also similar to Uncle Phil's actions after he saw his father crying in fear over his push carts again being destroyed.

Immediately after the murder of the bully, Grandfather could not understand why he was suddenly given preferential treatment at the Washington Market. He was also offered the choice pushcart locations at the busiest street corners even when he was not there first. He could not understand where all the newly given respect came from. People who never even bid him "bongiorno" now greeted him warmly and gave him gifts. "What a wonderful country", he must have thought. He began to respond by giving away spoilable vegetables that were left over after a day's work.

Young Uncle Phil never said much about what he did, but was relieved when no gang members came to exact revenge. It was soon realized that there was no gang willing to take on the notorious Livoti/Simone family from Mazzara San Andrea. After all was it not a known fact that if a person ever insulted them, their women would shoot you dead from the balcony? It was also known that if a man made a pass at a widow from this family, then her son would shoot him dead too. Uncle Phil had committed his first of many murders, only one of which he would be found guilty and serve time in prison. I think after the murder of the bully, Grandfather eventually got the idea why he was suddenly treated with such respect. No one ever knew of a discussion between father and son on this matter. It was soon noticeable that all members of Carmelo's family were treated with respect.

Along with his five sons Great-Grandfather Filippo Neri had three daughters. I mentioned Great-Aunt Concetta and the demise of her first husband under a balcony on the streets of Mazzara. He also had Great-Aunt Rosalia who went on to marry Giovanni DiLorenzo. They too lived on Elizabeth Street but also purchased a bungalow at 101 Winham Avenue in New Dorp Beach, Staten Island. I remember that summer home with its verdant grape arbors, friendly dogs and endless mosquitoes. We used a marinade to rub on our arms, legs and necks. It was made of olive oil, vinegar and garlic to keep the annoying flying insects away. This concoction was also worthy when splashed on salad. Another effective mosquito repellent was a smoke screen of burning cattails. We called them punks. I wondered if this was the way frogs lived in Sicily, always having to resist the vermin of the swamps.

♪♪♪♫

Great-Grandfather's other child was my mother's Aunt Candida for whom she was named. She was one of the only female members of that family that was educated. I remember her as being matriarchal, respected by all my aunts and uncles, possessing great wisdom and having huge breasts. Everyone called her Zia, which means, *aunt.* Somehow, this was bastardized into "Titzi." As a child I always thought she was called that because of her womanly endowments. It was Great-Aunt Candida to whom all members of my family turned to for advice. She was referred to more formally as Zia Candida which was bastardized into,

"Atsa Gandia." Other names I remember whose pronunci-ation was changed to conform to the Sicilian dialect were Tsuano for Zio Gianno (*Uncle John*) and Tsu Datsio for Zio Oratzio (*Uncle Horatio*). As a child, when I ask about these burdening life mysteries, I was given the bathroom expla-nation. The word for bathroom in Sicilian is *bachowsa*. This was derived from the term 'back house' which was the form of sanitation used at the turn of the last century when the immigrants arrived in America. Thankfully, that explanation cleared up a muddled mystery for me.

Candida Livoti was married to Pasquale Leonti. He owned and operated a successful Italian restaurant on Elizabeth Street. It had a reputation for excellent steaks. There were wire-backed chairs with hard round seats and red and white checkered tablecloths. The floor was of small hexagon shaped white tiles. I remember being told stories of how corrupt New York City policemen, (who were always Irish), would come to his restaurant to shake him down for money and a free meal. At the time the Italians were the newest immigrants singled out for abuse by the Irish. The Irish were the previous immigrants, and became the civil servants of the day. Being Italian was to be referred to by these previous immigrants as "WOP" which is an acronym for "without papers."

Whatever was served to the bullying police, Great-Uncle Patsy would always add a distinctive ingredient. The food never left the kitchen until Uncle Patsy endowed it with a mild flavor of nicotine and wine delivered from his contemp-tuous mouth. I was told he always accentuated the act with a loud, "*touhey.*" I am sure a, "Disgrazia, Bastardo," or a "Figulo de Puttone," was added for good measure.

Tia Candida Livoti Leonti

In addition to the steaks, Uncle Patsy was known for his great wine. Once as a young boy, along with my older cousins Angelo Pernicone and Bobby Scialla, we found several barrels of fermenting wine. It was in the garage located in the rear of his huge Mediterranean house. The mansion had walls of beige stucco and a green Spanish tile roof. It was located in Oakwood, Staten Island. I remember sucking from hoses inserted into the barrels to sample Uncle Patsy's wine. To this day, I have not tasted wine as good as that. We were caught and since I was the youngest, I got the blame for coming up with the idea.

Great-Uncle Pasquale Leonti had a sister Angela, also from Mazzara San Andrea. It was common for families to arrange marriages then. This was an occurrence of a brother and a sister from the Leonti family marrying a brother and a sister from the Livoti family. At the age of 15, Angela Leonti was sent to America to marry Carmelo

Livoti. He was ten years older than she and was a cousin through marriage. She had red hair, blue eyes and fair skin. Because of her unusual (for Sicilians) complexion and she hated the sun. Sicily, having been conquered by invading armies since the beginning of time is said to possess a mixed gene pool. My grandmother's physical characteristics give credence to the theory that among the island's many conquerors were the Normans. Grandma lived with us for the first 12 years of my life. She spoke no English but she was my second mother and I loved her dearly. When I asked her if she ever wanted to return to Sicily, she reacted with anger indicating she was still mad for being sent here to marry a stranger at such a young age. Also, she said she was painfully sick during her long sea voyage to this country. I suppose she was disenchanted at being widowed at the young age of 39 with eight children.

I wonder if her courtship went any better than her mother's. When her parents were married her father, my Great-Grandfather Leonti, had his arm in a sling. It had recently been broken by a smash from a kindling log. It seems that the prospective bridegroom took an excessive liberty while sitting by the fireplace with my soon-to-be Great-Grandmother. He foolishly placed his hand on her knee while they were engaged in raucous laughter. The soon-to-be bride immediately stopped her laughing. She was responding to the unwritten Sicilian Code which had been taught to her since her early childhood. There is an unwritten rule that dictates a woman must never allow freedoms to be taken with her body until she was married. She promptly picked up a log and punished the offending hand by breaking the arm to which it was attached. Good thing the ever present Sicilian family shotgun was not handy. If it were used at this episode, then our genetic chain would have been broken. None of us would have been born.

꩜꩜꩜

After the deaths of Mom and Dad in 2009, and the sale of their house, I came across interesting memorabilia. Among them were autograph books from their graduation from elementary school. Mom graduated from PS 21 near their Elizabeth Street home. I was impressed at how many inscriptions were written in Italian. Because Mom's father had died two years earlier, her oldest brother Phillip assumed the role of head of the family. His inscription in her autograph book reflected that leadership role.

I found it interesting the differences in the culture we live in now and that which existed for my parents. In this next page from Mom's autograph book we see one of the numerous inscriptions written in Italian.

Uncle Patsy, who had a successful restaurant business on Elizabeth Street, felt a patriotic duty to return to Italy and fight in World War I. He was assigned to an Italian unit in the Alps that was tasked with holding back the British. He often spoke of the hardships and hunger. When his unit was relieved and he had access to food, he prided himself at being able eat "una kilo" of pasta. When we kids realized that one kilo was equal to 2.2 pounds, we had a new-found respect for Uncle Patsy who was my Grandmother Angela's brother. He was also an uncle from two directions because he married my Grandfather, Carmelo's sister, Candida.

Another aspect reflected in that immigrant culture was the use of nicknames. There is one from Mom's cousin

Inscription in Mom's Autograph Book, 1931

Salvatore 'Sam' DiLorenzo. Sam was a hero to me. He took me hunting in upstate NY and to Maine for deer. We often hunted rabbits and pheasants with his wise hunting beagles on Staten Island. Also, we would haul his small boat on top of his car and troll for striped bass and bluefish off New Dorp Beach. Sadly he died at the age of 44. Sam's death was the first death of someone I knew and loved. I was deeply saddened by it. A heavy smoker, Sam died of lung cancer. Since that loss, I always had an aversion to cigarettes and cigarette smoke. I even became intolerant of other smokers, often telling subway, bus, and ferryboat commuters to put out their cigarettes.

Today, we live in suburban neighborhoods. We are friendly with our neighbors. We discuss the weather, local public works as it affects our daily lives, sometimes even politics. Back at the turn of the last century, as the immigrants began to live in groups they were familiar with, there was a deeper bond formed among neighbors. They lived

Uncle Pasquale Leonti

much closer together, often eight families in one building each threatened by the same beast, that of their economy. They did business with those who were their close neighbors and treated each other like family. One notable family that lived in 238 Elizabeth Street was the Cappas. In Mom's autograph book, I found five entries made by that family. There was Luca, Marie, Frances, Salvatore and the only one I, and much of the movie world knew, Katherine. Katie, as my mother called her, married Charles Scorsese. Their son went on to become one of the greatest filmmakers the world has known. One of his first films, *Mean Streets*, was shot in the very neighborhood he grew up in, Elizabeth, Mulberry, and Mott Streets.

When Martin's father, Charlie died, he secured the entire old Saint Patrick's Cathedral for the wake and funeral. I remember bringing my parents to that beautiful church to pay our respects. When Katie saw us she insisted we sit with her in the first pew. I remember when many well-known movie personalities came to her and treated us like close family. Robert DeNiro, offered his condolences to us. My son Alex, who was with us, was enthused as he identified Isabella Rossalini after she greeted us.

When Martin Scorsese was filming, *Cape Fear* in Florida, Katie called my mother and invited them to the location of the filming. My Dad was on in years at that time and didn't feel up to the drive of more than two hours to the movie set. They did visit the Scorseses in the posh New York City apartment that their successful and loving son Martin, provided for them.

*The Palazzolas, the Pernicones
and the Scorseses, 1939*

⟩⟩⟩⟨

In 1931, Great-Uncle Patsy Leonti and Great-Aunt Candida Livoti bought the large Mediterranean style house in Oakwood Heights, Staten Island. It was of frame construction with tan stucco walls, brown window shutters and it had a distinctive Spanish tile roof. The master bedroom had pocket doors with brass handles, the living room had a brick fireplace and the interior was trimmed with chestnut molding. The furniture included Chippendale chairs and there was artwork, statues, and sconces, all imported from Europe. The Victorian decor was so authentic, the entire house could have been used as a movie set. The upstairs area included three bedrooms, a huge bathroom, and a kitchen. The typically Italian-American basement also included a kitchen and was the location of all holiday and weekend family dinners. Of the eight Livoti children, six were married, and of those five had children. It was not uncommon for 25 place settings to be arranged on makeshift tables snaking around that huge basement.

I remember everyone always happy and the dinners being a time of great excitement. Uncle Patsy, sitting at the head of the table, would get drunk and, in broken English, tell us about the time he fought the British in World War I. He would, in his animated way, explain how, after being rescued from a remote area without food or supplies for a week, he ate, "una kilo" (2.2 lbs) of pasta by himself. Then his other favorite story was about the time he saw Mae West in a live performance. He then would stand in his place at the head of the huge table and with his hands in front of his chest, bounce her enormous but imaginary breasts in his hands. I remember his eyes being wide open from the excitement of telling the story and then opening his mouth and closing his eyes as he enjoyed the memory. My mother and aunts would all yell at him from the embarrassment at hearing such bawdiness.

The detached garage located at the end of a long

Pasquale and Candida Leonti's Home
Oakwood Heights, Staten island

driveway was huge and modeled as a miniature version of the house. It had huge wooden accordion folding doors and housed six wine barrels along with tools for every use. As a child, I remember the long 1936 Buick, which had running boards and was a shiny black. There was an extra pair of seats in the back that folded away when not in use. The rear yard was equipped with a chicken coop and rabbit hutches. I remember the concrete patio area and the Victorian wrought iron furniture. The table was round with a thick glass top.

Above the patio were two huge trees whose broad leaves created a protective canopy like a green umbrella. One was an elegant magnolia, the other a lofty mulberry. The fruit of that prolific fruit tree attracted legions of songbirds. Our constant companions were robins, catbirds, mockingbirds, thrushes, blue jays and blackbirds. Without their raucous calls, my childhood memories of that magical yard would have somehow been less enchanting. The chickens and the

Joanie Scialla on the Patio, 1940

feeding songbirds attracted various hawks. When we spotted a plundering raptor, Bobby would run for the single shot .22. By the time my cousin would return with the rifle, the hawk would be gone, carried out of range by a summer thermal current. In that early pleasant time of my life, hawks were the only threat we children knew.

The rear of the house was filled with a thick growth of deciduous trees that grew unimpeded for several miles, all the way to Richmondtown. Aunt Candida and her sister-in-law Aunt Rose would take us children for long summer walks in the deep woods searching for the numerous

The Livoti Girls, 1940

mushrooms that abounded there among the ferns nestled between the brooks and ponds. The fragrance of those deciduous woods has never been duplicated for me.

From my earliest memories of childhood, I remember my father saying that June is the most beautiful month of the year. I remember those words as we admired Aunt Candida's flower garden which was intertwined with elaborate brick paths. I remember my cousin Joan, Bobby's older sister, saying that the iris is the most beautiful flower in the garden. To this day, it remains my favorite. Among those peaceful childhood memories there was a dog that I loved. He was part chow, all black, and his name was Skippy. He was always busy digging in mysterious holes around the chicken coop. Occasionally, with a wrinkled brow, and one ear that could not stand completely erect, he would proudly show us the fruits of his labors in the form of a dead rat.

I also remember the primitive circle of stones in the rear of the yard where my aunts and mother would grill magnificent steaks that Uncle Jimmy, Angelo's father would bring from his workplace. He was a butcher. It was also a common habit after dinner to burn all garbage in that same circle of stones. It was exciting to watch as the hypnotic lighted wooden match was placed at several locations on the garbage bags so several columns of fire could begin their destruction at once. We children would imagine the burning bundle as Hitler's house and would applaud as it became consumed in flames.

I always loved animals but because we lived in Brooklyn I couldn't have one. We rented an apartment in Borough Park and a dog would not have fit in. It was a Jewish neighborhood and dogs were not part of the landscape there. A dog on 48th Street between 9th and 10th Avenue was about as common there as a camel. One day I remember making a trip to mother's cousin John Livoti's chicken market in Coney Island. It was there that I was given my first live warm-blooded pet. It was a young black and white rabbit.

We were on our way to Aunt Candida's house in Oakwood on Staten Island and the rabbit remained on my lap the entire trip as I sat in the back of my father's 1934 Dodge sedan. It was then in that hour-long ride that I bonded with my pet rabbit. The hutch, located in the rear of the huge Mediterranean house, was where my rabbit would live. I named him Thumper. He would be happy there among the singing birds, tall leafy trees, and woodland scented breezes. I would spend hours at home thinking of Thumper and his comfortable home.

We would spend weekends playing the various adventure games that the deep woods in the rear of the house would invite. My cousins Bobby Scialla and Angelo Pernicone were older than me and omniscient. They were my best friends and being older than me knew everything there was to know about the world.

They were much better athletes than me. Angelo who lived on 48th Street, a block away from me and depending on the season, was always the shortstop or quarterback on our Brooklyn neighborhood teams. He was wiry, muscular, had a great arm and speed. He was a charismatic leader and was always our team captain. Bobby was also a great ballplayer. He played varsity baseball for New Dorp High School and today is a par golfer. In those days I only remember trying to swing a too-heavy bat and striking out.

Among our many adventures at Aunt Candida's Oakwood Heights home was exploring the abandoned Elks Club Mansion located at what seemed a continent away. Exploring that collapsing rotting building was a great fascination to us. The dank smell of mold only added to the excitement of the youthful adventurers. There was an orchard of pear trees in the rear of the building which was the home of many challenging out-of-reach pears.

During the baseball season we would watch the baseball games played at the Elk's Club's baseball field. The home team was the *Riviera Chateau*. We always cheered for them. The players drank water from a metal pail and all shared the same ladle. When the water would run out or get too warm, Bobby would run the pail over to the faucet in the Negro cemetery adjacent to the ball field to fill it. Angelo and I always accompanied him with that task of great responsibility.

The Elks field had a flat infield but the grass in the outfield would get fairly high on occasion. If the ball wasn't watched closely, the game would stop and it would take both teams, along with the spectators, searching in concert, to find it.

In 1948 my father and Uncle Sam Palazzola became partners in an eight millimeter home movie system. I remember the first films of a baseball game at the "Elks." Uncle Sam would film the hit and the race to beat out the throw to first base. In order to conserve the very expensive film he would not waste footage on every pitch. He would begin filming only after the batter swung and hit the ball. It appears was though there was great pitching that day because the entire reel shows batters running full speed only to be thrown out at first base. As time went on Uncle Sam Palazzola and my father became more accomplished cameramen. We kids appreciated the Saturday afternoon matinee at the Lane Theater in New Dorp, much more than home movies. Roy Rogers was our favorite hero.

Uncle Sam was also a gifted craftsman who built and flew "U" Control model airplanes on the Elks field. I do not believe the Wright Brothers were more excited than us on those sunny summer mornings when Uncle Sam flew his planes.

On the next trip to Oakwood Heights, I couldn't wait to see Thumper. I rushed back to the hutch and was disappointed when I couldn't find him. I asked my Aunt Grace, but somehow she didn't hear me. I asked Uncle Bob, Bobby, and even Aunt Candida but somehow I always became distracted and never got an answer. The first real shock of my young life came the next day. I happened upon a strangely familiar animal skin hanging from the ceiling and drying in the boiler room. It had black and white markings and was

Uncle Sam Palazzola, 1944,
Before Leaving for War in Europe

Cousins Angelo, Me, Bobby, 1945,
After Uncle Sam's Return From Europe

larger than I remember. I wasn't sure at first but it could be Thumper. When I asked everyone what happened I somehow again was distracted and didn't get an answer. I then became certain of my beloved pet's fate.

The lesson I learned from that incident was that dogs make much better pets than rabbits. From that day on I couldn't wait to become a dog owner.

CHAPTER **13**

From Russia and Delancey Street With Love

I also had the family history of my father's family passed on to me over the years. My Dad's father was an intelligent and powerful man. It was said he possessed great strength. He appeared at carnivals performing strong man feats. Based on what was told to me about him, I wrote this following story as to an episode in his life.

Abraham Finkelstein sat cross-legged on the curb with his hand holding his head, palms over his ears. He rocked slowly. The dead man lay a few feet away near the curb on Delancey Street. The Irish New York City policeman with his oversized handlebar mustache had his hand on Abraham's shoulder and was talking softly to him. The cop was treating him with an unexpected kindness. "That'll be awlright meboy, I sah the hull thing, you were not to blame," he heard the policeman say.

He would have been treated much differently in Russia if this had occurred there. Had a Jew killed a Russian like

*Abraham and Rebecca Finkelstein
and Children, 1909*

this in the old country, it would have gone badly for him. If
he ever survived the beating of fellow Russians, and was not
executed by the government, he would be sent to the salt
mines, never to see his family again. All Abraham did was
to slap the teamster in the face as an automatic reaction
to being hit in the face with the blunt end of a horsewhip.
He never intended for the man to move his neck in the way
of his hand. Abraham couldn't remember slapping anyone before. To illustrate his gentleness, I remember his son
Izzy telling the story of how he would gently lift the cat off
the kitchen table when it licked the butter. But then he was
never hit with a whip before. He couldn't understand the
kindness of this policeman who was as Irish as the corpse.

"The dead teamster," he despaired, is laying right here
at my feet on the cobblestones of Delancey Street, Oy if
he would just go away." If this would all just go away," he
wished. If he only had a chance to do this day over again
he would apologize to the man driving the beer wagon.

He would apologize for having his cart filled with the garments he was wheeling to Orchard Street being struck by the huge beer wagon with four horses speeding on the late afternoon crowded Delancey Street. If only he could do it over again.

What about his recently arranged wedding and his new bride, the tiny Rebecca Tulchinsky? What would she think of him now? Oy, what trouble he was in. What shame he brought upon himself. He began to wonder where the salt mines were in America.

He thought back to his youth working on the farms in Russia. He would carry two 40 kilo flour sacks, 100 American pounds, on his shoulders from the mill. Sometimes, to impress his fellow workers and the foreman, he would place a third sack across the back of his neck. He had such great strength that a circus passing through his town of Uriv, offered him a job as a strongman. He could do circus stunts like bend iron bars, lift a cow, hang from a rope by his teeth and impress all in the audience. His Uncle told him he had inherited the strength of Samson. He performed in his home village but refused the offer to travel with them because he didn't want to leave home.

Abraham changed his mind about leaving home when he heard of Russia's war with Japan. He knew that he was of the right age to be drafted and he knew because of his reputed feats of strength he would be among the first to be taken away. He had nothing against the Japanese, he never even saw a Japanese person. The answer was for him to travel to America and make a new home.

He seriously questioned his decision to leave Russia after riding for an hour in the dung wagon. He thought he would die under the weight of the stinking, damp blanket, of manure. He allowed himself to be hidden there by Saul the Smuggler to make the border crossing out of Russia. All he kept thinking, while gasping for breath, "What a load of shit I am in."

Now he was sitting on this curb in his new land thinking, "Now I am in another load of shit." He was fearful of what was to become of him. "This is such a beautiful country, there are so many opportunities to make a living, and now this," he lamented.

Police Officer Patrick Mulcahy NYPD saw the incident. The bully, Sean Mulligan, had been many times in front of the desk at the Elizabeth Street station for beating his wife and kids to bloody pulps. He was often accused of using his horsewhip on hapless pedestrians too. Now, he would never strike another being, neither man nor beast. Today he hit the wrong man. "This wiry Jew is one strong son of a bitch," the policeman thought. PO Mulcahy would make a full report to Captain O'Malley who was a fair and just man. He was certain that no charges would be brought against this sad, thin Jew. The poor bastard, he was in the wrong place at the wrong time. This hard working Finkelstein was on the same street as this reckless Mulligan. All the Jew did was slap Mulligan in the face. Is it the Jew's fault if Mulligan decided to have a heart attack today? PO Mulcahy was certain the good captain would see it his way. Fortunately, the good Captain O'Malley agreed with him. The bloody festering sores on the backs of Mulligan's unhappy team of horses were a sad reminder of the bruises on the faces and bodies of the bully's wife and kids. This was proof enough of the kind of man Mulligan was. He got what he deserved; he picked on the wrong man today.

Abe and Rebecca's Children 1944
Izzy, Gussie, Barney, Eva, Willie, Alex

Among the many eyes watching this incident was Carmelo Livoti. He stood frozen in place at the side of his pushcart. He was in his favorite spot on the South Side of Delancey Street. He admired the spunk of the Jew when he struck back at the disgrazia Irishman. Carmelo also felt a sense of compassion for his fellow merchant when he saw the tough-looking Irish cop appear on the scene. The feelings of alarm and pity for the Jew soon changed when he saw the policeman treat the gloomy man with kindness. His expectation of an arrest and rough treatment did not occur.

Maybe the Irish weren't all bastado. Maybe there was hope in this city. Carmelo Livoti could not wait to get home tonight to tell this story to his wife Angela and to his Sicilian neighbors on Elizabeth Street. He wondered if they would believe him.

CHAPTER 14

A Boy's Travel Journal

The previous mentioned Closet Elves must have felt generous because I found Alex's journal. The following is the
journal that my son kept on three of our summer trips to the
Rockies. It consists of 13 wrinkled legal pad pages and is
unedited. They began in 1979 and continued in 1981 just
as they were written by a boy when he was 10 and 12 years
old in a moving vehicle. Sometimes he wrote on bumpy dirt
mountain roads, but mostly we rode the interstate.

1979

*At 6:10 AM on the 28th of June 1979, with an odd license
plate number, a half tank of gas, we started off on our trip.
We were in Darth Vader, our new 1978 black Chevy van.*

*We filled up in a Pennsylvania gas station in the country at
95 cents a gallon and no gas line. It was foggy and chilly.*

*We stopped for breakfast at a Stucky's at 8:45 AM. I
had pancakes and orange juice and dad had pancakes
with two fried eggs on top and coffee.*

Very light traffic, corn is about 12 inches high.

10:34 AM it's starting to rain.

At 2 PM we took the first exit off the Ohio Turnpike for a gas station but it was closed. About 5 miles later, at the next exit there was 5 gas stations, one is open and at 82 cents a gallon we have the fifth place in line.

On the Ohio turnpike there are many rock stations and they are excellent. In parts of Pennsylvania we couldn't even get any radio stations so Dad played Willie Nelson tapes.

In 1973 when we drove to California with the whole family, Dad told me the Ohio Turnpike was foggy and hazy. In 1977 I remember the Ohio Turnpike was foggy and hazy. Now, in 1979 it's still foggy and hazy. Each time we have been here the sky was white. It seems you can never get sunburn here.

All cars from Pennsylvania, New York and New Jersey, seem to have even numbered license plates. Except us. We have an odd numbered plate.

We are now on the Indiana Turnpike. I thought it was 3 PM but it is really 6:45 PM. I must have been asleep for a while. Indiana smells like rain.

We just saw our fourth 18 wheeler turned over on the side of the road. Maybe it was done by the striking truckers. Last year we didn't even see one wrecked truck. So far we saw one in PA., two in Ohio, and one in Indiana.

It happened that way going west.

It's now 9:45 PM and under an orange crescent moon, I saw a large black bird flying. It was probably an owl.

The corn in Iowa is 18 inches high. The weather at 8 o clock in the morning is better than Ohio. The sky is blue with puffy little clouds, the sun is bright and the air is dry and cool.

At 10:45 AM CT, a rust colored sedan with six old people in it went into the left median, did a 180 degree turn and traveled east in our west lane. That was at the 430 mile marker on I-80 in Nebraska.

It happened that way going west.

At 11:32 CT, a lone mourning dove tried to cross a piece Nebraska land. While traveling from north to south it passed front of us traveling east to west. It struck our left front windshield. He left some blood, body fluid and feathers with us. He is probably dead now.

It happened that way on route 80 going west.

At 3:11 PM we are 40 east of Ogallala and a bee flew in the window and stung my father's back.

It happened that way on route 80 west.

June 29th 5:30 PM MT, we went to the Crystal Palace for supper. I had grilled cheese. Daddy had buffalo balls, in other words, mountain oysters. They were fried in batter. After we ate there was a stage show. It was made up of cowboys and saloon girls. They took me on stage. They sung me a song then they kissed me covering me with lipstick

Alex on Stage of the Crystal Palace,
Ogallala Nebraska, 1978

After the show we went back to our camp at Lake View Fishing Camp. At our site there were hundreds of toads hopping all over the place.

It happened that way going west.

At 10:36 AM MT, we crossed to Colorado borderline. We are on our way to see the Canhams in Castle Rock.

July 13, 1979 we left Castle Rock, CO. We said good-bye to the Canhams, those that were awake. Shawn, Timmy, Terry and their mother were still in bed. Their mother has been in bed for two days.

In Castle Rock we had a good time with the Canhams. We went snake hunting and camping with them. We went to Castle Rock and my father was on the radio station for playing his harmonica with Peggy Malone.

We went camping with the Canhams and we also went fishing.

Alex With the Canhams

Timmy and Pat caught two trout. One night we slept outside and saw the Skylab. The next night, at the same time, we saw it again. In the morning we heard it crashed near Australia.

It happened that way going west.

July 13, 12:05 PM MT, and just left Cheyenne, WY. My father was getting me a knife and was testing to see if it was safe, and he cut his finger.

5 miles east of the Kings Row Restaurant, we saw a carcass of a steer by the side of the road. It looked like it was eaten by coyotes. Very close was a herd of antelopes. There seems to be a lot of them in Wyoming.

The Kings Row Restaurant was a dump. I doubt that any king ever visited there.

On the road to Flaming Gorge National Recreation Area, it's also called the Red Desert. We passed a dying desert snake. We backed up and watched him in his moment of death.

It happened that way heading west.

The campgrounds in Flaming Gorge were loaded with all kinds of wildlife. We saw ground squirrels, chipmunks, rabbits, antelope and an eagle. These were right inside the campgrounds. Outside the campground, we saw a pair of great horned owls. We met a girl from France. There was also a group of Germans singing all night.

It happened that way going west.

Our windshield got cracked by a passing car going fast over loose gravel.

We saw a big brown prairie falcon being chased by little birds.

On Friday the 13th, Daddy raised the flag over Cheyenne, WY.

July 16, 1979, today one of the days Daddy's digital watch was an hour slow. We rushed to get Willie to his roudez with the canoe filters? (illegible)

We went on a boring historical tour. We went into

Jackson, WY, had ice cream and rode the Alpine Slide. We drove to Teton Village and rode the tram. At the top of the mountain the chipmunks were hungry and climbed all over us looking for something to eat. The day isn't over because we are going on an evening hike into Cascade Canyon at Jenny Lake.

1981

1 August 1981, at 6:45 AM on Staten Island, my father cleaned the windshield and started the engine, he put Willie Nelson's, On the Road Again tape on and then we started the trip.

At 6:57 AM we got gas at Texaco. We filled up with lead free. It came to $15.00 at $1.57 a gallon.

We have been traveling for 1 hour and 20 minutes. We are in Pennsylvania now on Route 33 North heading for Interstate 80. Nothing exciting happened yet.

At 8:30 AM we got on I 80 West. We are going to take this all the way to Ogallala, Nebraska.

At 9:20 AM we stopped at Stuckeys. At 10:00 we finished breakfast. We bought some nuts to make gorp.

We saw two dead deer. They were at the side of the road squashed.

That's what happened on route 80 west.

At 2:40 PM we went under the Ohio border line. It happened that way on route 80 west.

At 2:57 we are running out of gas. We might not make it to the gas station. But it looks like we will. It happened that way on route 80 west.

We're getting off at exit 10 to get something to eat and get gas. The gas was $1.26 a gallon here. We traveled 439 *miles since the last time we got gas, it came to $14.70. We aren't eating here because it looks cheap. As we were driving out we saw a groundhog.*

It happened that way on route 80 west.

At 3:30 PM we stopped to get lunch. We saw a man there with a pet fox. At 4:00 PM we started on our trip again.

It happened that way on route 80 west.

Every time we go through the Ohio Turnpike the sky is always white, it is cloudy and it is humid but not bad on pollution.

It happened that way on route 80 west.

Traveling on route 80 west at 4:53 PM I looked to my left and there I saw buzzards soaring looking for something dead to eat.

Corn is 3 feet high in August. In Indiana it is the same size.

At 6:45 PM we stopped for ice cream.

At 7:10 PM we were at the end of the Ohio Turnpike. Then we entered Indiana. My father greeted it with a sneeze.

It happened that way on route 80 west.

Indiana is 170 miles long. We will be through it in 3 hours.

We have traveled in one day what took us in 1973, two days.

At 7:50 PM my father decided we should get some gas. We stopped at a Standard gas station and got it filled up with no lead. It came to $12.00.

It happened that way on route 80 west.

In an hour and 45 minutes the odometer will switch to 10,000 miles at 8:21 PM it just changed to 9900 miles.

At 8:27 PM CT, we left the Indiana turnpike we missed the time zone change sign. The cars clock and my father's wrist watch is one hour fast.

2 August 1981, at about 9:00 AM we stopped to eat breakfast at a McDonald's right near Council Bluffs, Iowa. We mostly drove through the night. We stopped at a rest stop once.

We're in Iowa now. I didn't write much before because I had stomach aches but I am better now.

We just past under the Nebraska border line. At 5 or 4PM we should reach Ogalalla and we are going to sleep in a hotel. Then at night we will see a show.

It happened that way on route 80 west.

Last night we slept for 3 hours at a rest area, and then we stopped again for 1 hour. Right now we are traveling west in Nebraska. It's about 11:30 AM and I am going to sleep.

It's about 12 noon and we are stopping for gas at an Amoco station.

We got unleaded, it cost $14.00.

The corn is about six feet high here. It's as tall as my father.

3 August 1981. Last night we saw a show in the Crystal Palace in Ogallala. We slept in a hotel. By this afternoon we should be in Denver, Colorado with the Canham's.

Its 10:10 AM and we are leaving the hotel and are back on route 80 westbound heading towards Denver where we will be staying. We just saw a little bird chasing a hawk.

Last night, my father, once again for four years in a row, had mountain oysters or you can call them buffalo balls.

At 10:40 AM we crossed the Colorado border line.

It happened that way going west.

We're in Castle Rock now and we just saw the Canham's old store. We are going on the dirt road to find the Canham's house. It is 20 miles inland and I hope we don't get lost again like we always do trying to find it. I just got a new pen and combination beater spreader and spatula from the nice old man that worked in the gas station. So far it looks like we are on our way to the Canham's. We're starting to get lost on these dirt roads. We are now lost. My father is starting to remember the way there. Now, he doesn't remember any more. We definitely are now lost. We are starting to remember the way. We are now at their house.

9 August 1981. We left the Canham's and we are passing through Worland at 1:20 PM to go to the Grand Tetons with Zeke and Greg.

At 5:50 PM MT we see the Grand Tetons, at 5:57 we just pass the Grand Teton Nation Park border.

18 August. At 2:50 PM we get into Pennsylvania.

All 3 years when we came back it has been ugly, but this year it is very nice weather. At 8:00PM we are saying goodbye to route 80.

That's what happened on our trip out west.

CHAPTER 15

On the Road Again

I am driving on the highway again. This time my vehicle is headed towards Florida. After a 10 year gestation period, *Highway Odyssey* has resumed its tale. I suppose it was Willie Nelson's, *On the Road Again* that came on my radio that gave my psyche a kick start but as I searched for I-95 South somewhere past Norfolk, I became motivated again.

There were no satellite radios or GPS navigation systems when I started this writing and there was always Dad to read my daily creation of words and make comments. But now so much has changed. Every day since his and Mom's deaths I realize how much I miss them.

Max, my black, 80 pound, energetic, standard poodle, and I were taking the eastern route through Delaware, Maryland and the Eastern Shore of Virginia. That would take us over the Chesapeake Bay Bridge and Tunnel system, about 18 scenic miles over Chesapeake Bay. When I made this trip with Mom and Dad we always made a rest stop at the restaurant in the middle of the water on that magnificent ride. It afforded delightful views of the Chesapeake Bay and its and shoreline. Sometimes there were fish jumping. Once we watched a huge naval submarine headed out to sea. There were always colorful and energetic shore birds. That October of 2001, was at the height of the bird migration and ruddy turnstones, in their glorious plumage, were scattered everywhere along the rest area. Walking back to the car in the parking lot, Mom stopped and noted their beauty.

Upon reaching the southern end of the Chesapeake Bay Bridge and Tunnel system in Virginia Beach, I had to look for the route that would lead west to Interstate 95. There is always heavy traffic there and I am always anxious about it. Now, in fall of 2009, I have my GPS guidance system to plan the route and trip for me. However the GPS, with its awesome technology and its infinite wisdom decided to route me southward on a modern six lane, with a huge divider in the center. At first I was delighted that modern technology found a better way for me.

The first rest stop Max and I visited was in the Dismal Swamp and was like a scenic park. There was a pond with picnic tables, doggie bags provided on a pole and wooded trails. Wow, Max and I were in heaven. We hit two rest stops with these great displays of nature. Max, with great interest began to leave his scent and like his predecessor Ava, a powerful female Rottweiler. Max scratched mini trenches with his rear claws, for all fauna to remember him by. Then very gradually I noticed Route 17 beginning to lose its width. First the scenic, center island disappeared, then there were fewer lanes and then it was a narrow two lane road. This was disappointing and scary because I didn't know how long my GPS was going to lead me through this terror.

❧❧❧

Two-lane country roads brought back the unpleasant memory of a day in the summer of 1973. Irene and I took the five kids on a cross country drive in our 1969 Ford Country Squire station wagon. We had just left the Howards in Hudson Colorado and continued our journey to Davis, California to visit John Carroll, Irene's brother who taught at UCD. From there we planned to visit her Uncle Vincent Carroll and his family in Palos Verdes Estates, a posh area on a cliff overlooking the Pacific.

We were about a half hour west of Hudson on a two-lane road when a dump truck, driven by a dude called Big Red, passed us going East as we traveled West. At the precise time that our two vehicles passed each other the huge truck's oil cap decided to shake itself loose and strike our windshield. We were going 60 miles per hour in one direction and Big Red in his massive red dump truck was doing at least 60 mph in the other direction. That created a missile traveling 120 mph that hit us.

The impact was piercing. Glass sprayed all of us. There we were an innocent family of seven from New York. We were traveling West, minding our business and intent on getting to Salt Lake City, the next leg of our trip. Irene screamed that she was shot. She held her bleeding arm and I pulled over to the side. Big Red kept his easterly direction without batting an ignorant eye.

I got out of the car and retrieved the missile. In the midst of a large stretch of desolated country road, I recognized there was activity ahead. I vaguely recalled the red dump truck pulled out of that site. We put clean tissues on Irene's forearm wound and I drove to the busy, what seemed like a construction site. I later realized it was a quarry where rocks, not sure what kind, were being excavated.

There was an office trailer which I entered with red oil cap in hand and asked for help. The boss there, when I told him a red truck that caused our problems came from this site, took the situation very seriously. He immediately indicated that Big Red was the last to leave. He was quite helpful and after seeing Irene's wound and our broken windshield, he offered to take her to a hospital which she refused. He then offered to have our windshield replaced by the auto glass facility he dealt with. It was located in Fort Collins where we, at his direction went to. The repair people drove us to a mall where we hung out until the windshield was replaced in about an hour. I believe we were given top priority at the behest of Big Red's boss. I still think that company is happy that we didn't sue them for Irene's injury. To this day, 36 later, she carries that shard of glass in her forearm.

))).

I'm not sure when their dementia began. It was different for both of them but the ache of aging was a daily presence since maybe, the new millennium. Dad gave up his income tax preparation business and passed it on to me in 1998. That means he must have been feeling mental deceleration about that time. Although for the first three years I took over the business, he had every answer to every question I had for him, which were many from me in those early years of my tax preparation business. I was amazed at how he knew every one of his clients by name, address, the business they were in, their marital status and the number of dependents. He would be in Florida and I would call with a question, mention a client's name and he would rattle off all their details.

Dad's mind was amazing, it was like a calculator. I remember an incident 1986 when I had many renovations done to my Burbank Avenue home. I had an inch-thick packet of bills related to the construction items from various home improvement stores. I wanted to get an idea of how much I spent. Dad told me to read off the total on each bill. I did, and without a pencil, just adding each number in his head, with 70 or so documents, Dad added the number, $16,300. Later that day, at home, I checked Dad's number against my calculator and I got $16,292. I thought that was awesome. His mind was just amazing.

❧❧❧❧

I drove them to Florida in October 2001. I remember the date because there were a few noticeable changes. That year, Mom and Dad left their Staten Island home for their tropical winter roost, before voting. They always voted with great interest, and like their parents before them, always the democratic line. In addition, and I didn't blame them here, they didn't want to fly. It was just a few weeks after the horror of 9/11/2001 and the country didn't know when the next attack would come.

During that trip, Dad sat anxiously in the passenger seat barely leaning back with his hands tightly holding his knees. He intensely focused on the road as though it was he doing the driving. He would often point out that I was too close to the truck ahead. I wasn't, but he perceived that I was.

Dad on his Terrace in Hollywood, FL.

Mom was mostly quiet except for the times when we passed the shopping areas and discount stores in North Carolina. In addition, she gave a bit of family history when we passed, Cape Charles, VA. It seems her father leased land there to grow vegetables that he sold both retail and wholesale at New York City's, now defunct, Washington Market.

We planned on spending two nights sleeping in motels with the 24 hour ride spread out over three days. That made it a fairly comfortable trip.

⌇⌇⌇

Now, it is October 2009 and my travel companion is Max, loaded with about 800 pounds of raw energy. We will spend only one night in a dog-friendly motel. It will be a "Days Inn" in Florence, SC. Max has never been away from his Staten Island home. For the several week long vacations I took to come to the Florida condo and a flight or two to Colorado, he spent a miserable time at a kennel.

Later that year I found Bonnie Petit, a dog lover who boarded him in her charming Tottenville home. He was always happy at my return and always a few pounds heavier. Now, he was traveling longer than he ever traveled in his life, he was quite stressed as his third blood-filled defecation at the scenic overlook at the north end of the Chesapeake Bay Bridge indicated.

The night at the Days Inn was almost a disaster. Cursing the misdirection of the GPS, we got there two hours later than expected. I walked Max around the well-planted grounds, unloaded the Lincoln MKX and proceeded to settle in for the night. After a shower, Max took one bed and I the other and I was so tired I shut the light and began my journey into sleep, or so I thought.

It was 7 PM. Just as I entered into the REM phase, maybe 15 minutes, Max growled, barked and began to prepare for war. In the thin-walled construction of the motel it seemed other guests were checking in closing doors, turning on faucets and walking past our door. I soothed him and scratched under his neck, spoke softly to him and then crawled back into my bed. About five minutes passed, I began to relax and Max sounded off again. This time he leaped off the bed and charged the door. I contemplated packing the car and getting on the road and continuing on to Florida to do an all night, 24-hour, one-shot marathon ride to our destination. That was out of the question because, as Dad would say," I'm not as young as I used to be." In my weary misery, I thought of a way to mask the annoying sounds I turned on the air conditioner. It was old, noisy, and it worked. I arose to use the bathroom three times between 7PM and 1AM. Each time Max was lying with his head upright and staring at me. It was clear neither of us was getting any rest. I reloaded the car, ate another peanut and jelly sandwich, offered Max a bowl of dry food which he refused and set upon our southward journey on I-95.

The Interstate offers a pleasant ride at that time of night. There was barely another car on the road. I set my speed control for 65 MPH. The permitted speed was 70 and began a relaxing ride. I drank cold coffee still present from my Staten Island kitchen, ate another peanut butter sandwich but the yawning and fatigue began to set in. I made two more rest stops at areas located along the Interstate to walk Max and energize myself. It was useless and at 4:30 am, I pulled into a rest stop in Georgia, tilted my seat back and slept more soundly than I did at the motel. I had been driving a mere two and one half hours with eight more to go.

I awoke quite fresh and energized. I believe Max was far more comfortable in the car than the motel.

We crossed the Florida border just as the sun was coming up over the ocean. It was a refreshing sight. It rose at the same location in the spring of 1979 with my new Chevy custom van, Darth Vader, with the five kids and Ellen Harty, my girlfriend at the time. We were doing a marathon drive, nonstop Staten Island to Hollywood. We were all younger then but we didn't have Max. I believe he presented more problems for me traveling with me than the long road trips with five kids.

My folks didn't own the Victoria Towers Condo then, they had a one bedroom condo on the intracoastal side of A1A. Nevertheless, we spread out all over the floors in sleeping bags and had an enjoyable time. During that trip I took the kids to Fort Meyers on the West Coast of Florida to visit their Grandparents, John and Irene Carroll. While there we spent a day on the beach at Sanibel Island. I was a bit uneasy at first meeting with them. Their daughter Irene and I had been married for 15 years and had five children together. This was the first time I had seen them since the pain and emotion of the split. They were quite happy to see us and didn't raise an eyebrow when I introduced them to Ellen who had been a former math student of John's at Tottenville High School. When we left, I was pleasantly surprised when John called me aside, shook my hand and thanked me for bringing the kids to visit with them.

On that day on a Sanibel Island beach, we met up with the kids of Billy and Rosemarie Hammond. This summer at a family party at the house of Gina Scialla Orlins and her husband Jordan did I find out that Jordan came from Fort Meyers and was close friends with Billy Hammond Jr. and may have been present at that beach venture. Somewhere I have pictures of that reunion. There seen a happy group of kids, mine and the Hammond's along with possibly Jordan. That photo album is hidden by the Closet Elves along with a number of other treasures of mine.

CHAPTER **16**

Beginning of the End

It was December 13, 2009, a sunny Saturday morning when Mom called. She asked if I could come over to help Daddy get up from the floor. He fell, she said, and he can't seem to get up. When I heard that I recognized the symptoms of a stroke and immediately called 911.

As I hurried over to their house on Allison Avenue, a mere nine blocks away, I was so agitated I had to keep reminding myself not to have an accident. I got there before the EMS personnel and told Dad to remain on the floor where he was until help arrived. I sent Mom to get a pillow to keep Dad comfortable and give her something to do. While lying on the floor, I asked him to smile, he did, and it was normal. I asked him to stick out his tongue and it too was flat and normal. His speech was clear. He was even cognizant because when he heard the EMS sirens he mentioned how fast they got there, not realizing I called them before I left my house. I still had a sinking feeling that it was a stroke, maybe because I knew that was what his parents both died from. When the EMS arrived they performed the same stroke tests as I but since he could not function with his left arm and left leg he was immediately brought to Staten Island University Hospital North.

It was less than a week earlier that we had a 70th birthday celebration for me at the Staten Island Hilton Garden Inn in the Japanese Tea Room. There were more than one hundred people in attendance. All our family and many friends were there. Mom and Dad were so proud of their family that surrounded them. Little did we know that it would be their last happy weekend.

I stayed 18 hours with Dad in the emergency room until he got a room. He was probably examined by about 25 or more individuals. He had numerous tests, the CAT scan being the most telling. It showed he still had bleeding on the brain. Most of those eighteen hours were on a gurney in the ER hallway. It was crowded with patients, some of which were frauds that just wanted attention, a place to sleep or both. These were Medicaid people, those that never contributed a penny into their health care insurance but had the same benefits as Dad who worked all his life and received the same care as them. I was to experience more of these slugs in the following weeks.

The most memorable meeting I had at the ER was with the head of neurology. Regarding Dad, he told me, "I expect a full recovery." At first I felt relieved, but a few hours later as Dad's speech became more slurred, I began to wonder how that doctor could be so wrong. How, I thought, could a 94-year old, make a full recovery from a stroke? Sadly my skepticism proved to be correct.

In eight weeks Dad would be discharged from the hospital, tended to at home 24/7 by home health care workers, admitted to Eger Nursing home, admitted to Staten Island

University South and moved to Colonial Funeral Home with his final resting place in Oceanview Cemetery. His burial would occur six days after Mom was laid to rest.

Dad never knew of Mom's death, he never knew of the horror of her fall, of the splitting of her left leg from the knee to the ankle, of the entire tibia and part of the fibula being exposed. With so many tendons exposed it looked like a color medical textbook photo from Grey's Anatomy. He never heard the female EMS worker telling her male partner, "You don't want to see this," referring to the huge opening in her leg. As she cut away Mom's pant leg there was evidence of tissue stuck to the inside of her pant leg that "exploded" from her injury.

Dad never knew of Mom's pain or her congestive heart failure, or her and my insistence at abiding by her wishes and not using intubations to prolong her life during her last 11 days of life at SIUH North. She and I both knew the quality of life by living solely on tubes and didn't want that. I applaud her bravery. Nancy and Betsy, with their intense love for her, tried to get the medical staff to use the intubation techniques. As health care proxy the doctor asked me what was going on. I told him my daughters do not want to lose their grandmother. The doctor was aware of Mom signing the DNI document and her wishes, he just wanted to be sure the family was in agreement.

No, thankfully Dad never knew that I was spending my days and evenings traveling from the hospital with Mom and Eger Home to feed him because at this time he could no longer feed himself. He had trouble holding the plastic fork and moving the utensil to the food. In addition, he was uncoordinated when loading the food on the fork. But if he was successful at all of this, his hand could not find his mouth. I shudder to think of his frustration. He agonizingly attempted these simple everyday maneuvers but with little success. So, I tried to get to him for at least two meals a day. Nancy was always there to feed him lunch. Dad never knew it but when I wasn't there with him, I was holding Mom's hand in SIUH North where she was living out her last days. She would always ask if I had been to visit Dad and told me not to tell him of her fall. Just tell him I have a cold if he asks, she would say to me on two successive days. Dad didn't ask, all the while he was in the nursing home he never asked for her. I think his brain became overly bewildered when he moved into Eger Home. It was not a fun time for any of us.

I remember Alaina, in a way characteristic of a six-year, asking me during Dad's first hospital stay, we were in the hallway during visiting hours, "Is Grandpa going to die?" I was in the company of her two sisters, Alexa and Adriana and her cousins Sydney and Zoe who were excitedly chatting as they always do when they get together. I was stunned as they fell silent waiting for my answer. I remember my answer was a tearful one. "Oh,"

Alaina quietly replied. The other four girls seemed

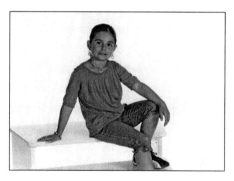

Alaina Scimone, Age Six

moved by my honest but sad answer. They spoke in quieter tones after that. I've since wondered if I was wrong in answering with such frankness.

Mom only got to spend 12 or so hours in the ER. It seemed odd that after a dozen or so doctors examined and tested her, I heard a familiar line from the same script. This time it was the head of internal medicine who said to me, "I expect a full recovery." What was that all about? Do they think if they revealed their true feelings it would be an admission of failure? Ninety-three-years old, with what was first thought to be multiple compound fractures, a history of heart disease and, I am told they expect a full recovery? It still baffles me.

Eventually it was congestive heart failure that got to Mom. Although, from the time I was told she might not last another 24 hours, she hung on for seven more days. She died February 12, 2009.

As I was driving into SIUH South's parking lot at eight in the morning to visit Dad, I received a call on my mobile giving me the news. I had to question the doctor because I wasn't sure who was resting in peace. At that time Dad was admitted the day before with pneumonia, sepsis of the kidney and necrosis. While in the nursing home one of Dad's toes turned black and I was told it would fall off. Thankfully he felt no pain there. Dad never complained of any pain, never, not ever, during his last eight weeks of life. That says a lot for his character. I believe he knew the stroke would be fatal. After all, his parents suffered the same fate, he had to know. The ER time must have been the worst part of Dad's ordeal. As his brain was slowly bleeding away his awareness, he must have realized the consequences of his affliction. As a young boy he lost his mother to a stroke.

A few years later his dad also died from a stroke. After he returned home, I remember the first time I took Max there. Dad looked down at Max, who was furiously licking the wrist of his immobile hand as it gripped the arm of his wheelchair, and said, "I can't scratch your neck, I'm sick now, Max."

I remember his recounting to me that as a six-year-old boy him seeing his mother's corpse lying on a bed of ice. It was a hot July Saturday and as a religious Jew she could not be buried on the Sabbath. In his autobiography, Dad wrote that she lay there in death, reclining on a bed of ice with one eye open, in their kitchen. He was terrified from that scene. So much so, that for many years, he could not go unaccompanied into their tenement apartment. He was a young child and alone and he feared the dark empty rooms of the tenement. He would wait for his father to come home from work.

It must have been a hardship for that young boy especially on Thursday nights when Grandfather Abraham attended union meetings and didn't get home until after 10 PM. Dad wrote that he waited for him, in the street, at the subway entrance. I can't imagine any of my children or grandchildren at six years of age, even being out alone, particularly at night and at a subway stop on the Lower East Side of New York. I shudder to think of the fear Dad must have felt as a child.

Similarly, when his father suffered a stroke, he experienced firsthand the debilitating effects of that medical cruelty. At that time, his married, older brother Barney invited him and his afflicted father to live into his large apartment in Borough Park, Brooklyn. Dad wrote that he used to walk his father to the barber for haircuts.

Dad must have known what to expect. I remember his silence while lying in that ER hallway, on that narrow gurney, with the beginnings of a slurred speech, he asked me what happened. I answered him that he had a stroke. Again, I wonder if I should have been so honest. I think so, because I would want to be spoken to honestly if I were in that condition.

As I write this now, I realize what he must have been thinking. Although he didn't show it, he must have been frightened. I wish I held him, reassured him more, I just remember telling him, "It will be ok Dad, it will be ok." Thinking back on it now, I wish I hugged him then.

CHAPTER 17

The Agony

December 13, 2008, the day of Dad's stroke, my children felt the enormous force of the bursting of the minuscule blood vessels on the left side of Dad's brain. Each of them stopped their Saturday duties and raced to New Dorp to be with Mom.

Dad's 94th Birthday at Carmen's Restaurant

There were significant signs of dementia for several years leading up to that day but the shock of it struck all of us like a lightning bolt. With Mom, it exacted its greatest toll. I remember my daughter, Eva, who along with Shalini, spent the day with her, telling me that I needed to get a 24/7 home health care worker to live with her. "Dad", Eva told me on the phone, I'll never forget the desperation in her voice, "She tried to heat a cup of coffee by placing it on the flame of the gas stove like it was a pot and she can't be left alone."

That took me by surprise, I always thought of her as my mother, who knew better than me and was far wiser than me. It was one of the many shocks regarding the changes that were to take place that day.

My daughter, Nancy stayed with Mom that night, and for the next few nights. It was a great hardship for Nancy because she has a household of animals to care for. She had several dogs and about 30 cats. She is an animal rescue person who recently formed a "not-for-profit organization," *Fur Friends in Need*. But Nancy stayed with Mom for the next 72 hours.

Then came Juliette, the Caribbean woman from Trinidad, whose English was as tangled as Turkish. That began a life of misery and disappointment for Mom. To have strange women in Mom's kitchen, cleaning her house and doing her laundry was too much for Mom to bear. My friend Sharon Pritchett told me of an Italian woman who I thought would be more acceptable to Mom who did home health care, but she was available. Thinking of it now, I don't think Mom would have accepted any person doing chores in her home, the household she was master over for 71 years.

A few weeks later when Dad came home from the hospital, I think the disappointment of not having things return to normal gave Mom the stress that eventually became her undoing.

After two weeks at home Dad proved such a stress factor to Mom. I had to have him admitted to Eger Nursing Home to get him away from her. She could not understand or deal with his deteriorated mental abilities.

After two weeks at Eger, Dad was admitted to SIUH South with sepsis of the kidney, pneumonia and necrosis of the foot. He lived only another 10 days.

On February 1, 2009, with Juliette's help, I took Mom to Eger Home to visit Dad. It was a Sunday and because we knew from the previous two visits to visit Dad at Eger, that Moms strength was failing. She complained his room was too far to walk to, it exhausted her. So, on this Sunday, I loaded Dad's wheelchair into the car and Juliette and I wheeled Mom to Dad's room. Since it was a Sunday, there were special events planned for the patients and their visitors. On that day, there was a jazz trio. Juliette and I wheeled Mom and Dad, each in their own wheelchair, to the entertainment area. It was a wide hallway with a beautiful view of the garden. As the trio performed, I watched as Dad whispered into Mom's ear, about things related to the show. As a child I remember him doing that when they took me to numerous Broadway shows. The music was entertaining for them, as they played numbers from the 1940's, an era they were quite familiar with. It was a shock and sort of cute to see Mom and Dad seated next to each other, wheel to wheel and hub to hub. Dad made comments as they did in their youth. I enjoyed seeing that interaction. I didn't know it then, but that would be the last time they would ever be together.

It was the following day that Mom fell down the front steps. Again, a huge change took place in our family. She would live only another 10 days.

My evening trips to Great Kills Harbor at Gateway Park would now only include Max and me. For the last five years, after eating dinner at Mom's I would take both of them along with me to Great Kills Harbor. I would take Max for his thirty minute walk and they would watch the sunset behind the picturesque setting of sailboats and seagulls. In the last two years I had to coax them more and more. I guess their energy was leaving them. In all that time I was successful only once in getting them to get out of the car and walking to a bench to sit. I remember it was a beautiful evening in June and the weather was delightful. I thought they enjoyed the view and clean air sitting where they could hear the seagulls and feel the weather.

Dad would walk every morning to buy the newspaper, risking life and limb to cross Hylan Boulevard, and thereby getting some healthy exercise in. Mom, on the other hand would only willingly walk if she were in a mall getting healthy shopping in.

One of the happy occasions Mom and Dad enjoyed was the celebration of Dad's 90th birthday. I have saved a collection of speeches, letters and handmade cards given to Dad. As I read these, I realize the full impact as to the many lives my parents helped to mold.

The following speech was given at the Hilton Garden Inn during a party on the occasion of Dad's 90th birthday:

GRANDPA

Thank you for being the grandfather you are, and always being there, for stressful times and for good times.

Words alone cannot express the gratitude I feel to have a grandpa like you. I realize how fortunate, I, as all your grandchildren, are to have you there always….I want to learn to be more like you…the truth is Grandpa, you always treat people respectfully, and hold them in high regard.

You have always worked so hard all your life, keeping your family's happiness as your priority. You focus on what matters and the goodness of life…

Today you are here in this world for 90 years, and experienced a life that your grandchildren never knew, and never will know. Maybe what you lived through is what makes you the special, generous and loving grandfather you are today. It has to be a wonderful feeling to experience a lifetime with your precious six great-grandchildren.

The one important fact I want you to know today, is that you are one of my favorite people in this world, and if this world had more people like you it would be a better place to live.

Nancy

ﭢﭢﭢ

Dad's stroke occurred six days after a family party we had at the Hilton Garden Inn on Staten Island. The occasion was for my 70th birthday. Mom and Dad sat proudly with me at Table #1.

The owners of that beautiful establishment are Richard and Lois Nicotra. They are former students of mine from

Susan Wagner High School.

I remember Richie as a student in my physical education class always having a legitimate excuse to get out of class to attend a student council meeting. As class president, he always had functions to attend. Knowing his aversion to P.E. class, I always let him go with a wink and a smile. Now, as owner of the most beautiful hotel, restaurant, catering establishment in New York City, I always use his services where we are well treated. They always showed respectful attention to my parents, acts of kindness I will never forget.

Richie and Lois Nicotra

CHAPTER **18**

Honesty and Integrity

On February 11, 2009, I received a call from Eger Home indicating that Dad was being taken by ambulance to SIUH South on Seguine Avenue. I was told he had pneumonia. Although I noticed his health and awareness rapidly dwindle since his admission to Eger home, I never had any idea he had pneumonia. I learned that his speech difficulties were called, *aphasia*.

Once, the day after the stroke, at SIUH North, he repeated to me, what sounded like, "Its twenty after four." Standing in front of him, I looked at my watch and said, "No Dad, it's only 12:30." His face registered frustration as he shut his eyes and shook, repeating, "Its twenty after four." I felt terrible that I couldn't understand what he was trying to tell me. I called the nurse who explained to me that it was called *aphasia*, which takes several forms. Sometimes speech is merely slurred, sometimes it is just unrecognizable sounds, and in this case his mouth articulated words that were different than what his damaged brain was intending to verbalize.

He spoke quite clearly in June of 1950 though. That was when I graduated from the 6th grade at PS 160 on Fort Hamilton Parkway in Borough Park, Brooklyn. I always remembered how proud he was as he said and wrote in my autograph book. Autograph books seemed to have gone the way of black and white televisions and Morse code. They used to be fashionable. When a student was graduated from school, whether it was elementary, junior high school or high school they collected autographs from family and friends. I have Mom's and Dad's high school autograph albums. I was touched to see my paternal grandfather's autograph in Dad's book. Abraham Finkelstein died long before I was born. *"To my beloved son Alex, I wish you biggest success in everything you start."* That is what my grandfather wrote to my Dad. It's the only thing I have from him.

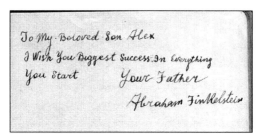

Written in Dad's Autograph Book

Sometimes it was just the autograph that people placed in the memory books, but most of the time the writer placed a pertinent phrase, poem or best wishes to the graduate. One of those was: *To Alex, Remember me first, Remember me last, Remember the fun in Miss Hall's class.* Your friend and fellow grad-u-8, Albert Tuber. Another one was: *To Alex-may your heart be as bright as Broadway at night-Your*

Abraham and Rebecca Finkelstein, 1919

fellow grad-u-8, Morris Nussbaum (himself." These were written in June 1927.

Dad would enter Dewitt Clinton High School a few months later. Clinton was located in the Bronx, a long distance from Borough Park, Brooklyn were Dad lived at that time. He traveled that distance on the subway every day because it was the elite academic school in the city. Because Dad was in a special scholar's program, he would graduate just two years later.

What Dad wrote on one of the pages of my autograph is something I will always remember. With microphone in hand, I repeated it in 2002, at the Hilton Garden Inn at their 65th wedding anniversary party. I did so for the benefit of my grandchildren because modernization now prevents us from the use of autograph books. **"As you weave your pattern of success through life, always use the basic strands of honesty and integrity,"** were his words I have never forgotten. It was the credo he followed and that I wish to pass on from him to my grandchildren.

On February 11th 2009, Dad was admitted into SIUH

South from the Eger nursing home. The next morning at 8:10 AM after I left Mom, after having visited her at 6 AM at SIUH North, I received a call on my mobile phone at the precise moment I was pulling into SIUH South to visit Dad. The caller identified himself and Dr. Somethingorother, a foreign sounding name with a thick foreign accent. It was difficult understanding him but I remember his words," rests in peace," I answered that I was in the parking lot and I would be right up to my father's room. He then said something else that was unintelligible to me and I asked, what do you mean by, "rests in peace"? Then I heard him say, "Died, passed away." I again said I would be right up and asked what room was my father in? He then said, "Not your father, your mother, she has passed and is now in peace." I told him I just left her; I had been there since early this morning and was at SIUH South to visit my Dad. When he understood, I told him I would return after I met with my Dad who was just admitted.

When I found Dad's room, I contemplated whether or not I would tell him. I decided I would tell him if he asked. Dad lacked awareness, his speech was distorted and I was shocked to meet the head of surgery who informed me he wanted to amputate Dad's leg. They had to evaluate the strength of his vascular system in his legs to decide whether or not to cut above the knee or below the hip. This was the second shock to me in less than a handful of minutes and I told them I would talk to him at greater length after I settle with my mother's situation.

I returned to SIUH North to Mom's room. I found Betsy there; she was standing at the foot of Mom's bed. Betsy's peaceful demeanor had a calming effect on me. I hugged her then kissed Mom for the last time and realized that this was the end of an era.

I knew I had to visit the funeral home and there would be obligations of mourning and burial. I knew I would have to notify family and friends of this final event. I also, remembered I had to notify the *Staten Island Advance* to arrange a proper obituary to chronicle Mom's life and her accomplishments.

Ocean View Cemetery had to be notified and the monument footstone to be placed at our family site had to be arranged. So many thoughts raced through my mind. All this seemed to be happening so fast. Then, with a confused sense of guilt, I felt relieved.

Mom was at peace now, her pain was gone. There would be no more of our pleading for the medical staff to give her more pain killers. There would be no more guilt of visiting one parent but thinking about rushing over to visit the other while squeezing in time to feed and walk Max. Those daily walks with Max, I believe had a cleansing effect on my muddled psyche. And now with the death of Mom, I was able to spend more time visiting Dad.

I never realized this new scenario would only last another eight days. Meanwhile as I raced towards the hospital to see Mom for the last time in a hospital bed, I was amazed that the world around me was so normal. The drivers, pedestrians, shoppers, busses, fire engines; all things went about their lives so normally. For me and my children, the world was different. We were encircled with confusion, uncertainty and grief.

Earlier that morning of February 12, 2009, as I stood next to my sleeping, heavily medicated mother, I looked out at the early dawn sky. It was blue and lightly flecked with grey clouds. I did wonder if the ominous black cloud that drifted over the Verrazano Bridge had any significance. I still wonder about that because Mom was in her last hour of life.

In those eight days which included Mom's wake and her funeral, I got to see Dad to feed him breakfast and supper. Again, as in Eger Home, Nancy was there to give him lunch. Shalini was also very compassionate; she always seemed to be around and helping. Dad's condition regarding pneumonia and sepsis of the kidney improved but the surgical team arranged to see me on two other occasions. The surgical staff was relentless in wanting to amputate his entire leg. It brought back memories of when Dad turned 65, the eligible age for Medicare. Dad called it the "Medicare Merry-go-round." That was when all patients of that magical age somehow were found to be in need of varied surgical procedures. In addition, numerous tests were instantly necessary. He felt that because the medical professionals would directly be reimbursed by the government, these medical procedures were "required."

In the nursing home, from their keeping him in a wheelchair 24/7 and their not permitting him to sleep in a supine position, he developed circulation problems in his foot. His toes turned black. One of the toes, I was told would self amputate. "It will fall off and be painless," they said. In recent years, Dad always had poor circulation in his feet. They were purple in color and the toenails were an opaque yellow. His left thumb toenail was a half-inch thick and that toe pointed straight up. I asked the podiatrist that Dad saw every six weeks about it. He didn't tell me much, but I assumed because he wasn't concerned, then I shouldn't be.

Curiously, it was the middle toe on his right foot

that was ready to fall off. His foot looked like that of a 6,000-year-old Egyptian mummy that I remember from the Metropolitan Museum of Art when I was a boy. That was on one of the many museum visits Dad took me to. As a fireman, he was often off during the day and would take me around the city where I was able to build many pleasant memories with him.

On 2/18/09, two days before his death, the surgical staff did their best to pressure me to allow them to do their amputation. I refused. I couldn't see putting Dad through any more discomfort, I was never told there was a direct relationship with the amputation and his immediate life. Nor was I told the surgery would be a cure-all for Dad's medical problems. I just didn't want him to suffer. I knew he was not suffering in the way Mom did and didn't want him to get to that condition.

That afternoon, I received a call from the hospital that they were going to discharge him the following day, 2/20/09. I was shocked, one day they wanted to amputate and the next day he was to be discharged. Knowing this I had two choices, one was to have him readmitted to a nursing home and the other was to bring him home and set up his Allison Ave house as a nursing home. I chose the latter. I was not satisfied with the care he received from his two-week stay at Eger. I, in fact believe they were basically responsible for his condition for not allowing him to sleep in a bed. Their reason was he would not stay in bed and continually tried to get up on his own. They, unlike the hospital, where not permitted to restrain him in the bed. I was told that nursing homes have federal regulations that prevent them from using restraints that hospitals are permitted to use. Also, they didn't have the staff to sit and watch him, nor did they have the staff to react to an alarm placed under his mattress that would indicate his getting out of bed. All of these strategies were denied to me when I requested them.

I remember so clearly, that day of having to arrange for a 24/7 nursing coverage, for a hospital bed to be delivered to his Allison house and to make a list of all other medical items needed. It was a monumental task which I undertook.

All my life I always remember Dad doing things that were sensible. In my adolescence, when I purchased my first car, a 1949 Chevy convertible for $150, I wanted to have it painted and dressed up at a far greater cost than the car itself, though it would not make the car run better. I remember Dad telling that was not a sensible thing to do with a clunker automobile. He said, "Your car should work for you, you shouldn't work for your car." Another sensible message Dad taught me was that your house is the best investment you will ever make, therefore you buy one as soon as you can. Unlike a car which depreciates with age, your house appreciates over time. So, any money put in to paint your house is well spent and an investment. Dad always had such sensible advice.

So my remembering Dad as being so sensible and him knowing (which I'm sure he didn't) that he was being discharged by the hospital, I was bombarded with thoughts that Dad willed his death to occur to make things easier for us. As though, in a last unselfish act, to avoid the problems connected with a move from his hospital bed in SIUH South, to hospital bed in the Allison Avenue home he loved so much. Could he have known of Mom's death through some surreal communication with her? Eva, thought so;

she told me exactly that, when she learned that Dad, in his semi-slumber state, would call Mom's name in his sleep. "Katie, come on, come on Katie," he called out on more than one occasion. Another time he called out, "Hurry up Katie, hurry up!" This happened when she was in her last days of life while under sedation and suffering from lack of oxygen due to her congestive heart failure. Eva believed they were communicating on some paranormal plane.

⌡⌡⌡

Dad was sensible all during his life, and now, this orphan child of the great depression, was sensible death's door. I believe he had awareness of the present circumstances and that on some intuitive level, he willed his death to make things easier for me and for him to join his wife of 71 years. As I write this, I am in the Hollywood Beach Condo now and Mom would be proud, I am sure. The tile man just arrived and handed me a bill. On it, an item that stood out amongst all the other items: It was the five-foot-long by six-inch-wide Sicilian marble sill. Sicilian marble in her bathroom; she would be so proud.

I have renovated the entire condo since their deaths nine months ago. I know Mom and Dad would be happy with that. There are two new baths, a new kitchen, and floor tiles. In addition, I had the textured "popcorn" ceiling removed and refinished. Also, the entire place was painted. The master bathroom was done with a walk-in shower. The Sicilian marble sill is to support of the shower doors.

I am the second generation as owner here at the Beach condo. And because of the barrier island resort location, on the same block as the beach and with a terrace that overlooks the Intracoastal Waterway and South Lake,

I hope to keep it in our family for generations to come. There are numerous restaurants of all styles within walking distance. Along with the bars and boutiques and the recently restyled Oceanwalk with its antique lampposts and trendy beach wall, makes this a pleasant vacation spot. In addition we are mere steps from the beach and its pale green Gulf Stream waters.

Mom and Dad have been coming here since 1977 when they purchased a one-bedroom condo in the Attaché Gardens on the opposite side of route A1A. They hung out on the beach here with a large group of friends, mostly from their old neighborhood in New York's Little Italy section. They would gather in the afternoon sun, on their beach chairs, with thermoses of margaritas and would decide what restaurant they would eat at that night. This close knit group of friends would arrange to take ocean cruises, trips to Europe, Las Vegas and Hawaii vacations together.

Among the many trips they took together was when they rented a Volkswagen minibus, and, along with seven lifelong friends, toured Italy. Dad kept a journal that depicts the fun they had. It is printed below.

Highlights of Italy Trip
Fall 1983

NINE DAYS WITH THE NOISY NINE or Sempre Dirite

- *Departing two hours late on Alitalia from JFK airport New York, the "Always Late Airline."*
- *Arriving at Milan to take our connection flight to Florence and discovering that it departs from another airport, more than one hour away. There would have*

been a 3 1/2 hour interval if we left on time.

- Learning at the service desk that she would change our connecting flight from the scheduled 12:30 PM to a 4:00 PM flight because there was insufficient time.
- Arguing that we had friends waiting to pick us up in Florence expecting us to be on the 12:30 flight. Obligingly and cooperatively she hurriedly has us find our luggage, had a porter zip us through Customs without inspection and then to a cab who literally "flew" us to the other airport getting us there with sufficient time, only to find out that our plane which was to take us to Florence had not even arrived from Florence yet.
- Night clubbing in Florence with Louie the leader dancing with his head on two pillows. (Louie Puglietti was an energetic but short man who enjoyed dancing with tall women).
- Shopping for goods in Florence with Adrianna driving hard bargains for the bargain hunters.
- Speaking of driving,-The Midnight Ride of Lou Revere_ "We are Lost," the captain shouted.
- Adrianna taking our expedition to a Pizza Parlor.
- Vonnie, amazed by it all.
- Squeezing ten pounds of potatoes into a five pound bag by loading nine people and eighteen pieces of luggage and bric a bracs into a Volkswagen minibus.
- Intrepid George trying to follow the road signs with the luggage rack cover flapping in the breeze.
- Lou, Von and Al trying to tie down the cover every thirteen kilometers.
- Our fearless leader Lou getting us through thick and thin and through water and fire with his wonderful native Italian diction when he was able to commander

the "Queen Mary" to float us and our baggage into Venice.

- The Noisy Nine never keeping quiet even when eating, and always eating and drinking.
- Vonnie enthralled by it all, on Cloud Nine.
- The "relaxed peaceful" atmosphere of San Marco Square.
- Sipping cappuccino and listening to music.
- The entertainment by the Venetian Opera.
- Vonnie enthralled by it all, engaging the local folk in conversation like he was a real Sicilian.
- Gina enjoying her presence in Italy.
- Chin chinning and Happy Hours-almost a happy for our leader.
- Louie with his convincing Italian dialect leading us out of Venice.
- Having prosciutto and cheese with a roll for lunch, on the autobahn roadside.
- Vonnie enthralled by it all. The four meals served up by Victoria's folks in Pescara.
- Always eating and always drinking and never getting to bed before the early hours of the morning.
- Grace and Sue enjoying the beauty of the trip.
- The rugged run through the mountains of Abbruzzes. A "Cliff Hanger."
- Kay and Al getting car sick in the back of the rocking and rolling minibus.
- Having lunch in a quaint mountainside inn with a flock of sheep passing in front of the window. Our fearless leader Lou getting us through with his conversational acumen and superb driving skills.
- Vonnie enthralled by it all.

- *Trying to break down the staid stuff atmosphere fo the Grand Hotel Ambasciatore in Sorrento.*
- *Getting seasick sailing to Capri.*
- *Chin Chinning through Happy Hours.*
- *Intrepid George maintaining our fiscal equilibrium while settling all the bills.*
- *Locating Francesco Rega's store and Francesco Rega taking us to a pizza parlor. Vonnie enthralled by it all, threatening to "end it all" when he returns to the States.*
- *Celebrating Vonnie and Sally's anniversary at the sidewalk café. The parting of ways. Sally excited at the thought of visiting her relatives in Sicily, two days sooner than planned.*
- *Gina becoming energized at the thought of visiting her folks in Campobasso.*
- *Lou, Grace and Sue heading for Campobasso, Pescara and Yugoslavia.*

Sicilian Campaign

- *Seven days in Sicily with four semi-Sicilians whose credo was, Chomping Our Way Through Sicily.*
- *Searching for ceramics in Vietri.*
- *Another Florence style, "lost our way, foul up" on the way to Naples airport. But for an English speaking local who borrowed a motor scooter and led the way to the airport, the Follow the Directions Four 9 (Sempre Dirtre) would still be in Naples.*
- *The ever present flies.*
- *The half hour discussion at the Catania Airport about putting up at a local hotel with Cousin Luigi by first*

taking us and all the baggage up to his fourth floor apartment.

- *Vonnie almost being driven into a ditch, barely five minutes out of Catania Airport by, "I can't see Cousin Luigi."*
- *Being forced, out of necessity, to take over driving a strange vechicle, in a strange territory, on a dark high, being directed by, "Che Benza Eio," Luigi to Luigi's home.*
- *Sally, Kay, and Al's cabby kept mumbling to himself, all the way.*
- *The superlative, overwhelming treatment given to us by Sally's relatives in Caltagirone.*
- *Vonnie enthralled by it all.*
- *The ever present flies.*
- *Eating mussels, pulled up by a rope, right out of Sicilian waters.*
- *Eating pulpe and dritz in Aci Terrisse. Eating and drinking and eating and drinking.*
- *Vonnie so carried away by it all.*
- *Being housed in the magnificent Caltagirone home of Sally's cousins, (Sallys cousins came to visit New York in 1977, their daughter's names were Concetta and Pippa Franco).*
- *The everlasting eating and drinking.*
- *Vonnie resigned to the fact that when he returns to the States he will have to, "call it quits," never being able to duplicate this life.*
- *The send-off of Sally's cousins on the Autostrada, as we departed for Taormina.*
- *The sky high ride to nowhere, in the dark, on the winding hairpin roads*

- *Taormina and points up.*
- *The ever present flies. The parting of our ways with Sally and Vonnie*
- *flying to Rome and heading home the next day.*

ↄↄↄↄ

It was an ideal retirement. Several of these friends lived in the Victoria Towers and told them when a two-bedroom unit on the fourth floor was for sale. They negotiated for it and the owner would not agree to Dad's terms.

A year or so later when another went up for sale, this one on the more desirable eighth floor, they pounced on it

Hawaiian Vacation.

So here I am now in the Florida condo, listening to the grinding away of the walk-in shower which is being redone for a second time because the misfit, crack addict, it turns out, back-pitched it. Meaning, when you took a shower the water gathered to the height of your ankles before it would start draining. Clearly, the floor was tilted in the direction away from the drain and not toward it. Duh, what was that guy thinking? He explained he was "sick." "Sick," I learned, is a euphemism for strung out on drugs. I was later told he used his drug of choice was crack.

Most of the renovations here at the beach condo were done when I was in New York. Not being on the scene to oversee the work was clearly a detriment. Since much of the construction work force here is not the highest quality, I was left with a few moments of anguish. My cousins, Denise and Charles Mistretta suffered the same stress when they renovated and decorated their condo in nearby Hallandale Beach.

CHAPTER **19**

Grieving

I don't know when it really started. I am referring to the deterioration of Mom's and Dad's abilities. I remember one New Year's holiday, while walking the Oceanwalk with Dad in Hollywood, Florida that Dad was bent over and seemed shorter than me. I had always recognized him as taller than me. His gait seemed slower and I realized he was aging when he cut his walk short and turned back long before we reached Johnson Street. I continued on with my run but felt that something had changed something I was not comfortable with. That was in 1998. I was 60, he was 84.

Also with Mom, that was the year that she made one of her famous dishes which was inedible. She had a way of preparing delicious Portobello mushrooms that could pass for filet mignon. She used fresh garlic and finely chopped onions frying it in a pan. It made the house smell great. It was always superb and fooled me into thinking it was the most expensive cut of steak.

On this occasion, I had just arrived from the airport by

cab, which means it was in the late 1990's because before that they would come to pick me up. I sat at the kitchen table for lunch. I took one bite and had to spit it out. It was like eating pure salt. Mom was always quick to defend any criticism of her cooking. I remember as a boy, her mother would get insulted if I ever picked up any seasoning to put on her food. Grandma always felt she did it so well it didn't need any enhancements. On this occasion Mom didn't say a word, she just took my overly salted omelet and quietly went about opening the refrigerator and getting the egg box to do another omelet for me.

I was somewhat shocked, I wondered if the top of the salt shaker accidentally fell off or maybe she shook on garlic salt instead of pure garlic powder. I think that was the answer because the same thing occurred in their Staten Island home a decade later. That was in 2008, a year or so before they died. At that time I was more cognizant of their dementia and tried to follow up on these sad mysteries. On one Friday when Mom prepared a fish dinner, again the fish was inedible due to it being overly salted. This was quite a bummer because she was great at preparing fish. Like the Portobello mushrooms, her fish was excellent. She used oregano, garlic, and pepper baking it after a drenching in olive oil. Again the house smelled great from the aromatic blend of her spices. By process of elimination, I was able to solve this mystery. I realized she was using garlic salt thinking it was merely plain garlic. I solved that problem by discarding that item. An inedible meal due to over salting never happened again.

For a decade or so, I felt depressed from the implication of their dementia setting in. I think I started grieving that winter back in 1998 while walking with Dad. It was then that I saw their future of forgetfulness, bad decisions and physical frailties.

On one occasion when I was driving Dad to the audiologist and Mom wasn't around he informed me that he didn't have depth perception while he drove. This was evidenced by his loudly reacting that I was too close to the car next to him after my parking in the medical office's lot. He said he couldn't open the door because I parked too close. I walked around and easily opened it. I'm sure he was embarrassed and disappointed with himself when he saw that he was wrong. I felt so bad at that incident. If I could get a do-over, I would have adjusted the car to accommodate his anxiety. It reminded me of him telling me a few years earlier that getting old was tolerable, being old was the problem.

I told him I didn't think he should drive anymore that I would drive them anywhere they needed. Dad appeared relieved. When I got a buyer for his car it was Mom's strong reaction that emotionally cut me deeply, "You are going to make me a prisoner," she screamed one gray afternoon in front of her house. It even hurts me to write of this painful memory now. But their 1999 white Lincoln with less than 15,000 miles on it was sold. It was a relief for me but also an event of great sadness. We were witnessing the decline of an era.

It began for them before WW I; they passed their childhood during the roaring 20s, and came of age during the Great Depression. They met, courted, married, and bore a child, all during this era. In that time, they enjoyed the pop culture of the day. Clark Gable, John Garfield, Fay Wray, James Cagney, Mae West, Al Jolson, Frank Sinatra, Bing Crosby, Tallulah Bankhead and Greta Garbo were part of their lives.

Dad landed a highly coveted job in the late 1930's with the United States Post Office. With few jobs available, a highly coveted civil service position offered steady work and security. In a short time Dad replaced that job with one with the New York City Fire Department. The pay there was higher, much higher. They got an apartment in Brooklyn and proceeded to live a happy life.

Their working days were eclipsed by their retirement life. They took over a dozen memorable vacations in Europe. At times they were accompanied by Mom's sisters, cousins and friends from childhood. It was an ideal life. Getting old was a blast, being old was the problem. Dad's words were so true.

Somewhere in the 1990's, I had thoughts of the time of my parent's deaths.

I thought of Dad being left without a mother when he was a just a child. Every child had a mother. I reflected on what his mother thought when she was near death, knowing she was going to leave her young son behind.

Rebecca Tulchinsky Finkelstein was devout in her Judaic beliefs. Her male newborn was circumcised by a Moyle according to her religion as were her other three sons. Her other sons had their bar mitzvahs and upon their deaths someone would say kaddish, the Hebrew prayer for the dead.

I remember Uncle Barney and Uncle Izzy's funeral services. I always thought when Rebecca was drawing her last breaths if she wondered and worried of her son's future. I made a decision long before Dad's death that I would see that the prayer would be said for him. It was more out of respect for the religious beliefs of the mother he knew for just a few short years and the grandmother I never knew.

In the early 1990s, while still a teacher at Susan E

Wagner High School, I asked Steve Lerner, a friend and colleague if he knew a rabbi who would do that. He informed me that a rabbi wasn't necessary and he would be glad to say kaddish for my father when the time came. On the morning before Dad's burial, Steve came to the Colonial Funeral Home and said kaddish, the Jewish prayer for the dead. I am sure Rebecca knew and was pleased.

In that time, Mom suffered greatly from the changes that began on 12/13/08 with Dad's fall in the kitchen. She showed signs of forgetfulness and confusion to an extreme degree. Nancy slept with her for the first five nights and then an array of home health care workers arrived which became part of Mom's misery. They took over her kitchen. Even though Mom couldn't handle normal mechanical functions, like turning on the stove or washing machine, she abhorred the aides. The aides also did her laundry. I remember Mom complaining to me she didn't want them washing her clothes; she wanted me to get rid of them. It was a difficult time because I knew they were needed. Again, I recalled Dad's words of a decade ago, "Getting old is acceptable, being old is the problem."

Dad's physical and mental decline was like a slow leak on a tire, Mom's was like a blowout. In eight days she was dead. Mom had a fall down the front brick steps on Monday February 4, 2009; the following week she was gone, her life was over.

All their lives both Mom and Dad were like Ferraris and Porches, fine-tuned racing machines that rarely stuttered, missed firing or hit bumps. It was heartbreaking to watch them fall apart.

I recently watched an old black and white movie from their era. It was a Daman Runyon drama starring Henry

Fonda and Lucille Ball. It was a tragedy about a night club singer, the Lucille Ball character, who treated everyone with contempt. Henry Fonda was a smitten busboy who would do anything for the singer. The story had the singer fall into bad times when she had an accident and became a paraplegic. The busboy did everything he could to keep the crippled, but still nasty, singer happy. In the end he arranges a huge party allowing Lucille Ball's character to sing and, with his help, dance for the last time.

The last lines of this drama struck me deeply. After the infirmed singer took her dying breath a friend said of the busboy said, **"A citizen never loses what he has filed away in his ticker."** I felt that way about of my parents. They touched so many people, from the friends on the Florida beach, to their neighbors, all their family members. They will always be in our hearts.

Dad, Me and Mom
We Never Lose What Is Filed Away in Our Hearts

CHAPTER **20**

Semper Fidelis

It's still 1999 and I am approaching I-78 as I enter New Jersey. I have just come through a powerful thunderstorm and again, I feel safe in my comfortable 1999 Lincoln Continental which is pulling my Harley Road King. The bikers heading home from Sturgis are fewer. During the storm I passed a few wet bikers taking refuge under highway overpasses.

After the intensity of the storm, my brain has somehow begun to relax. When this occurs I often think of incidents in my past, I'm not sure why, maybe it was hearing Mama Cass singing, *Words of Love*, but I am brought back to the 1960s and my time spent on active duty in the United States Marine Corps.

I entered Long Island University as a freshman physical education major in the fall of 1958. Within a few months, in February 1959 I joined the USMC Platoon Leaders Class program. I would spend two six-week sessions during my freshman and junior years at Quantico Virginia to receive recruit training. Upon graduation I would be commissioned a second lieutenant in the U.S. Marine Corps Reserve.

Aboard the USS Okinawa, 1963

The two training sessions were quite memorable. Much has been written about the recruit training depots at Paris Island and San Diego California for enlisted recruits. The treatment of officer recruits was no different regarding the shock, degradation and punishment of the recruit. I remember that July day in 1959 being singled out for some infraction and being made to hold my 9lb. 8 oz., .30 M1 Garand rifle at arm's length. When, after what seemed like an eternity, my arms began to sag, and the lieutenant in charge, while heaping significant verbal abuse upon me, struck me under my elbows which resulted in a long-lasting, painful tearing of my deltoids. That was not a fun day.

This incident occurred on the rifle range after qualification. We had to have photos taken for the hometown newspaper. We stood at attention in line waiting our turn to sit in front of a stretched-out old glory background. Our harassment was nonstop and this even went on during this photo session. One candidate, for some reason drew the ire of the lieutenant in charge and was made to retake his photo with his silver helmet liner worn backwards. I thought that was hysterical and could not keep back a visible snicker.

The lieutenant immediately charged at me hitting me with his chest and began his harassment with the extended rifle routine. It ended when his ego was bolstered and he was satisfied I was properly disciplined and suffering long-remembered physical pain.

Another occasion, far more humorous, occurred after noon chow one hot humid Camp Upshur day. Due to its primitive physically demanding daily routines, we recruits soon learned to call it Camp Rupture. Knowing how hot it would be during the afternoon's marching exercises on the drill field, I secreted a small carrot out of the mess hall. It was found under my pillow and I was singled out as a common thief of government property. The mess hall rule that we could take all the food we wanted from the chow line but had to eat all that we took. A drill sergeant stood by the trash can to ensure no government food was wasted. A day didn't pass without the drill instructor forcing a candidate to eat his leftover food he intended to discard. In my case I hid the carrot in my pocket to chew out on the hot drill field hoping it would relieve my thirst.

In front of the platoon, who was told that thieves were to be imprisoned, I was led away. I was brought to the Quonset hut which served as our company office. In front of two other smirking DI's, I was led to a wall locker and told to get inside. The metal locker door was slammed shut and I found myself crammed in a narrow, dark, metal box.

The office soon became quiet as the sergeants in there reported to their duties on the drill field. I didn't panic, I checked the time on my luminous dial watch, and it was 1240. It was hot in the locker and I felt comfort with the knowledge I had a full canteen of water complete with a sassafras twig. The woods of that part of Virginia abounded with sassafras. I remember impressing some of my platoon mates when I explained to them how to identify a sassafras tree. It's the only tree with three different shaped leaves. When you scratch the bark of a twig it smells like root beer. In addition, I believe it has a stimulating ability. I was not too uncomfortable in my dark prison and, in fact it was actually more comfortable than on the hot, humid drill field.

As I relaxed, I began to doze in my confinement. I soon became alert when the quiet the office was broken by the sound of the screen door opening and slamming shut followed by the distinct sounds of boot heels on the concrete floor. I became tense while in my slumped position, with my rifle in hand, web gear wrapped around me and my silver domed helmet liner cocked on my head.

The darkness of my confinement immediately turned to a harsh light. The gasp of shock and surprise from the drill sergeant broke the silence. "Vat da fuck," was his reaction. His speechlessness and look of astonishment was soon replaced with a knowing look of being had by his co-workers. When he regained his composure and fell into his DI mode he screamed, "Ged da fuck oud oof my logger you shid maggod." This DI was apparently recruited from the SS to punish future Marine Corps officers. This marine sergeant distinguished himself with a, quite natural, thick German accent. He was the DI of another platoon in my company and knew little of him other than he was loud and sounded quite mean.

I immediately ran from the office putting as much distance between the two of us as quickly as possible. As I regained my bearings I realizing I was used by my DI's to scare the hell out of a rival DI from another platoon. Once the understanding of the events of that afternoon hit me, I developed a new found respect for my drill sergeants.

I checked my watch and realized it was 1500 (3PM civilian time) and my platoon would still be on the drill field. I got to their location as they were taking a break under some trees that provided shade from the humidity and blistering sun. I was barely able to contain myself until I told my buddies what happened. I hurried over to their area to reveal my humorous tale. I also noted that my DI's observed my approach but never said a word to me. I am sure they were quite proud of themselves regarding the trick they played on their coworker. They wouldn't have to ask me about it. They knew they would hear it from their colleague. I wish I knew in what capacity he used a hapless candidate to retaliate.

As I passed through the 25-cent toll bridge over the Delaware River that bordered Pennsylvania and New Jersey, Willie Nelson was singing, *Angel Flying too Close to the Ground,* my thoughts reverted back to the great and wonderful men I got to associate with.

⟩⟩⟩

John Ripley, a Naval Academy graduate, distinguished himself at the Basic School and in Vietnam; I remember the PRT, Physical Readiness Test, when I couldn't beat his time in that three-mile run wearing full combat gear. I did well in the Obstacle Course competition but couldn't come close to John's run time.

John retired as a Colonel and for his actions in 26 major operations was awarded the Navy Cross, Silver Star, Legion of Merit (2), Bronze Star (2) and a Purple Heart.

His most notable action was the subject of the book by, Col John Girder Miller, *The Bridge at Dong Ha*. In that action which occurred during the 1972 North Vietnamese Easter Offensive, three mechanized NVA divisions made up of 200 tanks planned to cross the well-built bridge. The bridge that crossed the Cua Viet River was solidly constructed by our engineers for the resupply of Khe San. The NVA wanted it to fall like Dien Bien Phu, the battle where the French were defeated in 1954.

The NVA, North Vietnamese Army, needed the bridge for what was to be their planned conquering of South Vietnam in 1972. On April 2nd, Easter Sunday 1972, John Ripley had a different idea. While the NVA were on the north shore of the river, the ARVN, Army of South Vietnam, battalion which John was an advisor to, defended the south bank of the river. The ARVN unit was no match against the three mechanized divisions bearing down on them from the North. John had to destroy the bridge. He had 500 lbs. of TNT and C4 explosives which had to be strategically placed under the powerfully built bridge. It took John more than three hours, swinging hand over hand under the girders, while under fire from the NVA on the north bank to place the explosives. He had to make numerous trips to get the explosives, primer cord and primers. While on his first trip he realized he didn't have a crimping tool. This is a tool that crimps the blasting cap, which is a metal cylinder about the size of a thin cigarette. One end of the primer is open to receive the end of the primer cord to which it is to be attached.

In order to properly attach the primer to the primer cord, a crimping tool is necessary. Under the stresses of the battle, this tool could not be found. These are pliers with indentations in the squeezing blades so too much pressure would not ignite the explosive cord. Without the tool, John had to improvise and use his teeth. Biting too hard on this explosive could prove disastrous to John's health. He had to attach the primer cap to the clothesline-like primer cord to effect a simultaneous detonation.

Among the problems facing John was the NVA firing at him while he traveled hand over hand under the bridge and the subsequent ricocheting bullets aimed at him. He also suffered from the fatigue of scrambling using mostly his fingers to hang from.

Just imagine John Ripley's stress level. There was the NVA shooting at him as he hung under the bridge, he had three mechanized NVA divisions with their 30,000 men bearing down on his location from the North, and he had to maneuver under the bridge without any catwalks with his only attachment to the girders, the fingers of his hands. Ugh! In addition, he had to scramble back to the southern shore of the river to resupply with more TNT, C4 explosive, more primer cord and more primers. All this time he had to fight thirst brought on by fear, adrenalin and heat. There also was the element of fatigue in his hands and fingers from hanging and scrambling to strategic positions under the bridge to place the explosive charges in the positions to do the most damage to the structure of the bridge.

John was successful! He was able to accomplish his mission at the precise time the NVA registered its mortars on his ARVN battalion that was laying down a covering fire for him. John wondered, while running from the bridge with the NVA mortar rounds bursting all around him, if he did it correctly. His attempt to ignite the charge using electronic detonation failed. Wisely, John set a backup timer.

His doubts were soon dispelled when the concussion of his well-planned blast knocked him flat to the ground.

Under normal circumstances John would have been awarded the Medal of Honor, the highest award given to an American military person for actions in combat. Captain John Ripley was nominated for that honor for clearly he exceeded the necessary criteria. It was 1972; it was an unpopular war thanks to left-wing activists back home with their liberal media coverage. America didn't need media attention to the war or so felt the weak politicians in power at that time. Therefore, John had his award downgraded to the Navy Cross.

John died on October 28, 2008 at the age of 69. It was said to be of unknown causes. After the contact that many of our Vietnam veterans had with Agent Orange, the defoliant that was liberally sprayed throughout the front lines, sometimes right on our men, I am convinced it was the cause of John needing to have his liver replaced.

In addition to, *The Bridge at Dong Ha*, the book, *An American Knight*, by Norman J. Fulkerson is the story of John's life has recently been published.

In 2002, John was awarded the "Distinguished Graduate Award," the highest and most prestigious award given by the United States Naval Academy. In 2006, the Naval Academy Prep School in Newport, Rhode Island dedicated its new dormitory, "Ripley Hall," honoring their former graduate.

コ⊃⊃⌐

Now my thoughts are on a roll-back to my Basic School experiences. I am still on I-78 Eastbound and Willie is singing *Momma Don't Let Your Babies Grow up to be Cowboys."* Somehow my memory is drawn to Barney Barnum. Jeff Green, who was killed in Vietnam while searching for VC in one of their tunnels, used to call Barney Barnum, "PT." Jeff had a nickname for everyone. Ron Christmas was "Merry," Crockett Farnell was "Davy," I was "Flintstone"

Barney did get his well-deserved Medal of Honor. He was an artillery observer when the unit he was with came under heavy attack.

Barney's citation reads as follows:

For conspicuous gallantry and intrepidity at the risk of his life above and beyond the call of duty as Forward Observer for Artillery, while attached to Company H, Second Battalion, Ninth Marines, Third Marine Division (Reinforced), in action against communist forces at Ky Phu in Quang Tin Province, Republic of Vietnam, on 18 December 1965. When the company was suddenly pinned down by a hail of extremely accurate enemy fire and was quickly separated from the remainder or the battalion by over five hundred meters of open and fire-swept ground, and casualties mounted rapidly, Lieutenant Barnum quickly made a hazardous reconnaissance of the area seeking targets for his artillery. Finding the rifle company commander mortally wounded and the radio operator killed, he, with complete disregard for his own safety, gave aid to the dying commander, then removed the radio from the dead operator and strapped it to himself. He immediately assumed command of the rifle company, and moving at once into the midst of the heavy fire, rallying and giving encouragement to all units, reorganized them to replace the loss of key personnel and led their attack on enemy positions from which deadly fire continued to come. His sound and swift decisions and his obvious calm served to stabilize the badly decimated units and his gallant example as he stood exposed repeatedly to point out targets served as an inspiration to all. Provided with two armed helicopters, he moved fearlessly through enemy fire to control the air attack against the firmly en-trenched enemy while skillfully directing one platoon in a successful counterattack in the key enemy positions. Having thus cleared a small area, he requested and directed the landing of two transport helicopters for the evacuation of the dead and wounded. He then assisted in the mopping up and final seizure of the battalion's objective. His gallant initiative and heroic conduct reflected great credit upon himself and were in keeping with the highest traditions of the Marine Corps and United States Naval Service.

In addition to the Medal of Honor, Barney received the Defense Superior Service Medal, the Legion of Merit, two Bronze Stars and a Purple Heart.

Like John Ripley, Barney is a true hero.

There were other distinguished fellow classmates, Ron Christmas, Harry Blot, and Jim Brabham. Each of them went on to become Lieutenant Generals, that is, three-star generals. They were all in "B" Company, The Basic School 1-63. It was even more amazing that they were in the same training squad.

ᴗᴗᴗ

Ron Christmas is another hero from Basic School Class 1-63; he received the Navy Cross. His citation reads as follows:

The Navy Cross is awarded to Captain George R. Christmas, the United States Marine Corps, for extraordinary heroism while serving as the Commanding Officer of Company H, Second Battalion, Fifth Marines, First Marine Division in connection with operations against the enemy in the Republic of Vietnam. On the afternoon of 5 February 1968 during Operation Hue City, Company H was attacking a complex of buildings known to be an enemy strong point consisting of mutually supporting bunkers, fighting holes and trench lines. During the ensuing firefight, two platoons seized the corner building of a city block, but intense hostile small-arm automatic weapons, and B-40 rocket fire temporarily halted the advance. Realizing the seriousness of the situation and the urgent need to sustain the momentum of the attack, Captain Christmas, undaunted by the heavy volume of enemy fire, completely disregarded his own safety as he moved across the thirty-five meters of open area to join the lead element and access the situation. Returning across the fire-swept area, he rejoined the remaining platoon, issued an attack order, and then ran seventy meters across open terrain, ignoring automatic weapons fire, and satchel charges striking around him to reach a tank he had requested. Braving enemy fire and two B-40 rockets that hit the tank, he fearlessly stood atop the vehicle to direct

*accurate fire against the hostile positions until the intensity
of enemy fire diminished. Immediately realizing the tactical advantage, he jumped from the tank, and directed his
company in an aggressive assault on the hostile positions,
personally leading his men in room to room fighting until
the building complex was secured. In a large measure due
to his bold initiative and courageous actions, he provided
the impetus which inspired his men to aggressive action
and enabled them to successfully accomplish the mission.
By his dynamic leadership, unfaltering determination and
selfless devotion to duty in the face of extreme personal
danger, Captain Christmas upheld the highest traditions of
the Marine Corps and the United States Naval Service.*

Among Ron's awards were the Navy Cross, the Defense
Distinguished Service Medal, the Navy Distinguished
Service Medal, the Defense Superior Service medal the
Purple Heart, and the Vietnamese Cross of Gallantry with
Palm.

Ron went on to be promoted to Lieutenant General.
He is now the president and CEO of the Marine Corps
Heritage Foundation.

꙰꙰꙰

As I continued my Eastward direction into New Jersey,
my thoughts continued to swarm around the friends I knew
during the Vietnam War. Gary Arabian, was the first sergeant under my command after I left Basic School. He
impressed me like no other marine. Gary joined the
Marine Corps toward the end of WW II. He was part of the
invasion of Okinawa. During the Korean War, Gary was

a member of the First Marine Division that raced to the Yalu River. They were then swarmed over by the Chinese Communist Army that entered the war to assist the North Korean Army that our marines were crushing. The tide was turned and the First Marine Division became trapped at the Chosen Reservoir, North Korea.

In sub zero weather, unable to be resupplied they were low on food, ammunition and medical supplies. Unlike the 8th Cavalry Regiment of the 1st Cavalry Division who were unable to maintain their unit integrity to their western flank, the First Marine Division maintained their unit integrity and fought their way south to be safely evacuated. Gary and his fellow marines endured that horror and fought his way back while maintaining military order and discipline. He never thought he would ever be cut off and surrounded by an enemy with superior forces again. He was wrong!

On his second tour in Vietnam, he was at Khe San, and again he was cut off and surrounded by a disciplined, determined and well-supplied enemy.

I maintained a close friendship with Gary since first meeting him in 1963. After my release from active duty, I became a NYC teacher with an appointment at Egbert Junior High School on Staten Island. In my correspondence with Gary, I told him I was planning to re-enter active duty because of the guilt I felt for my fellow marines in horrible combat conditions. Gary told me in the strongest of terms not to do it. He told me the political ramifications were like they were Korea. Our elected officials were restraining us from winning the war. He wrote me that I had to think of my children.

When Gary returned from his second tour in Vietnam, he had dinner at my mother's house on Staten Island. He brought his elderly mother, a survivor of the Armenian Death March. She told us the story that she was seven years old when the march began. She was in the company of her mother and grandmother. In the first days the Turkish soldiers raped and then killed her mother in front of her and her grandmother. A few days later, holding her grandmother's hand, they were forced across the border into Syria. They were met there by Syrian soldiers who then raped and murdered her grandmother. I can just imagine how terrified that seven year old girl was, who somehow survived the genocide and had to live for years in the squalor of refugee camps. I took notice, where like my Dad; here was another child who was orphaned. I was thankful my children didn't have that anguish to endure.

In my parent's dining room, Mom prepared one of her typical, multi-course, Italian dinners. Gary and his mother were amazed at all the preparation and work Mom did. They were further amazed when I told them she did that every Sunday. It was our family tradition. I think of it now, and realize Mom was the glue that held our family together all these years.

While sitting next to me, Gary told me of the battle stress at Khe San that existed where artillery dropped down on your positions for weeks at a time. He explained how, in their numbed condition, some young marines would carelessly walk along the crest of hills, thereby exposing themselves to enemy sniper fire or how others would go about their business without their helmets on. He told me of his frustration and how he would constantly scream at distant marines to get off the crest of the hill or to put their steel pots on.

He then asked my advice on property he was considering

buying in San Clemente, California. Gary said he never owned property and was apprehensive. I explained that in real estate, there are three important things to consider. The first one is location. The second most important item is location and the third element to consider is location. In other words, location is everything.

When I asked what the view was like he said, "not much." I asked, "When you stand at the front of the property and look straight ahead, what do you see?" Gary said, "There is nothing to see." "Well you have to see something, what is there?" "Nothing," Gary again replied. "OK," I said, "what is in front of you, trees, buildings, commercial property?" "Nothing," Gary said, "the only thing you see is the water." "Water, a pond, a lake," I curiously asked. "No," he said, "it's the Pacific Ocean." I nearly fell over, "You mean you have an unobstructed view of the Pacific? "Yes," Gary said but if you look down the hill you can see President Nixon's helicopter pad. "Wow," I exclaimed, "buy it, buy it Gary." He did and when I visited him there the following summer I realized the extent of the property and the fantastic views. To the West from his hilltop location,

With Gary Arabian, San Clemente, CA, 1988

he stared at the Pacific, to the East and South he saw the mountains view of Camp Pendleton. Several years later in 1989 when I visited him, he put his arm on my shoulder and said, "thank you buddy, you made me a millionaire, and some developer offered me a million dollars for my house. Why would I sell, where would I go, I love it here," he proudly told me. He is still there today.

I overcame my stateside guilt and remained as teacher and remained as one for the next 30 years. One of my positions was supervising an evening community center. I was running a program in a gymnasium in Egbert Junior High School, Midland Beach, Staten Island. Since my specialty was gymnastics, I was able to teach the local boys stunts on the horizontal bar. Among those boys was Ray Rodriguez. He was eager, friendly, and respectful, a perfect candidate to become a gymnast. Since I was recently released from active duty, Ray was also interested in my Marine Corps experiences which I shared with him.

Soon thereafter, Ray came into the gym one night and announced he joined the Marine Corps.

I corresponded with him through his stint in boot camp and afterwards. Sadly, our communication came to an abrupt end. On March 3, 1968 the *Staten Island Advance* obituary headline read:

Pfc. Raymond Rodriguez killed on patrol in Vietnam.

A mass for Marine Pfc. Raymond Rodriguez, 18, of Midland Beach, who died Feb. 19 in a Da Nang, Vietnam hospital just 47 days after arriving in that country, will be offered at 11 a.m. tomorrow in St. Margaret Mary's R.C. Church, Midland Beach.

Pfc. Rodriguez would have been 19 years old on August 3, was fatally wounded in the lower abdomen, leg and arm when hit by enemy fire while on patrol February 15.

A member of Company D of the 1ˢᵗ Battalion, Seventh Marines, he had enlisted in the service last July, just a month after graduation from New Dorp high School.

His permanent record at the school describes him as "a model student-ambitious, cooperative and well mannered."

Long active in scouting Pfc. Rodriguez was a member of Boy Scout Troop 25 of Midland Beach Moravian Church, and last April was granted an Eagle Scout award.

Pfc. Rodriguez was born in the Bronx and brought to the Island by his family at age two. He grew up in Midland Beach and attended PS 41.

Surviving are his parents Mr. and Mrs. Peter Rodriguez of, 187 Freeborn Street; two brothers. Peter Jr. now serving in the Navy at Newport, R.I .and Anthony, of the home address; three sisters, Mrs. Victoria Bearer of Mill Road, New Dorp, Carmen and Caroline and a maternal grandmother Mrs., Carmen Gonzalez, also of the home address.

The Richmond Funeral Home, Grant City, is handling the arrangements.

On April 15ᵗ, 1968, nearly two months after reading Ray's obituary, I received a letter I had sent to Ray on February 12, 1968. It had a "return to sender" stamp on it. It took eight weeks and three days from the time I wrote that letter to Ray to get back to me. In that time, Ray was wounded in an ambush, his body riddled with AK 47 bullets, his unit fought their way out of the ambush, Rays bleeding was stopped, he was med-evacuated by helicopter to Da

Nang Hospital, and he lived five more days. His body was prepared, placed in a coffin, flown home to Staten Island, delivered to Richmond Funeral Home, he was waked, had a funeral mass said for him and he was buried in Moravian Cemetery.

Tears rolled down my cheeks as they blew taps that morning.

Via con Dios, Ray! I will not forget you and your noble sacrifice. You are a true hero.

♪♪♪

Paul Winters, a pseudonym, was a classmate of mine in PLC and in Basic School in Quantico, VA. We were released from active duty in 1965 and we both had interests in the FBI as a career. We were both interviewed and accepted in to the same FBI class at Quantico, VA.

For different reasons, neither of us started that class. Irene, my wife, didn't want to continue a military-style travelling life so I accepted a teaching position on Staten Island, a decision I never regretted.

Paul, code name Gung, in addition to the FBI, was accepted by the CIA and chose to work for the Company because they promised to send him to Southeast Asia. Gung, excited at becoming a "pop up" target for the NVA or Pathet Lao, volunteered for that immediate duty.

Following five months of paramilitary and operational training Gung was the only agent, from a group of 13, to be assigned to northern Laos. Gung, got to work with Hmong General Vang Pao. He was deeply honored and was raring to go.

Upon his arrival in Udorn, Thailand he was assigned to the current operation. Unfortunately, as a frequent visitor to the Air America Club, Gung was involved in a barroom fracas and was declared persona non grata by the club manager, a man with little humor.

Gung's boss, Karb, heard of the incident and abruptly ended his training period and immediately had him on the next plane to site 20A in northern Laos and the beginning of his 2 ½ year tour.

Gung's AO, area of operations, was the southern rim of the Plaine de Jars, a mountainous area with scattered outposts manned by Hmong irregulars armed with ancient M-1s, carbines and occasional 57 MM recoilless rifle and mortars. All of these were US military cast-offs from WW II. The NVA and Pathet Lao, on the other hand were armed with modern-day Soviet weapons.

One incident Gung remembered with interest was when he took an H-34 chopper to visit one of the outposts. To their great surprise they were greeted by heavy ground fire from a Soviet 12.7 Heavy Machine Gun as they approached at about 500 feet. The tracers were streaming all around his chopper and miraculously missed the cockpit and the rotors. Unbeknownst to them, the outpost had recently been overrun by NVA. Had they been permitted to land and had he survived the interrogation, Gung would have spent many years as a guest at the Hanoi Hilton. When he returned to base two clicks away, about twelve miles, the curious Hmong rushed out to search the chopper for holes.

A successful operation was immediately mounted to retake the outpost. While searching the bodies looking for intelligence, Gung removed an AK-47 from one of the bodies as a souvenir. Upon landing at their forward base, an Air America crew chief asked if he could have the AK and Gung happily gave it to him. On 12 January 1968, that AK would make history. The North Vietnamese had rigged an old Soviet Anotov AN-2 Colt biplane with bomb racks rigged for 120 MM motor rounds. The AN-2 made several bombing runs on site 85 called Phou Pha Thi occupied by three company men and several US military techs. In addition, guarding the site was a company of crack special ops Hmong troops. Site 85 was an important target to the NVA because it was the location of a TACAN (Tactical Air Navigation System) facility. This was a location where we controlled the navigation for the River Rats, the Air Force pilots whose targets were in the Red River Valley and Hanoi. An Air America chopper was working the area and moved to intercept the Anotov fixed wing. The Air America crew chief, Glen Woods, with Paul's gift AK-47, shot down the AN–2 Colt thus becoming the first helicopter in history to shoot down a fixed wing in air-to-air combat. A company team led by "Bag," was dispatched to the site of the downed enemy aircraft and they retrieved to body of the pilot. Not all of the body could be retrieved but Bag used his machete to extricate the main part. After some disappointments from their bosses, they sent the body to the American Embassy in Vientiane, the capital city of Laos. Amid laughter and a few beers, it was often wondered how they disposed of that partial body which was mostly the head.

Several months later the story had a sad ending. Glen Woods died in a helicopter crash while on an administrative mission.

Gung explained, to relieve boredom, he often took a Porter Stol Aircraft operated by Air America or Continental Air Services looking for NVA trucks or troop concentrations.

An occasion was recalled when a 37 MM Anti Aircraft gun opened up on their slow-moving 100 mph aircraft. The pilot seemed dazed and took no evasive action until Gung firmly slapped him in the back of his head and screamed, "Break right." Fortunately the explosive puffs were a thousand feet above them. The Pathet Lao gunners were obviously newbies and untrained in firing at slow moving aircraft.

One week after this incident Gung took leave and married the best-looking chick that worked in the American Embassy in Thailand.

Gung was a marine through and through. He suffered a disappointment with the powers to be at Headquarters Marine Corps Reserve. He was told he would be dropped from the Active Duty Reserve because he did not attend monthly meetings. Gung pleaded that he was indisposed because he occasionally was cut off from transportation. This was due to the NVA or Pathet Lao forces hunting him for the bounty on his head. He offered to go to nearby Vietnam to serve the Reserve's two-week required active duty time. Even though he completed the mandatory Marine Corps institute sub-courses his request was denied.

After numerous corresponding with the Marine Corps Reserve, Gung was told he would be transferred to the inactive reserve. Gung pleaded again that the war he was engaged in should be enough to provide the required points to maintain his status in the US Marine Corps Reserve. This time he was told that it was too dangerous in Viet Nam. Duh, didn't they understand who they were talking to? Apparently not, the USMCR transferred Gung out of the USMCR neglecting to recognize the incongruity of their denial.

Gung's final tour with the Company took him to Mogadishu, Somalia, four months after the Black Hawk Down incident which left the Somalis in an unsociable state. This precipitated the Clinton administration to call the expedition a tie and ordered all troops out of the country.

Upon Gung's arrival there were 1500 US military in the airport area and three weeks later there were none. The only remaining Americans remaining were 20 people assigned to the United States Liaison Office, (USLO), six of which were Gung's intel team. The USLO was not designated an embassy since one cannot have an embassy without a country to be accredited to. Somalia did not meet that criterion. The Brown and Root Company had a group of 50 supporting UN operators. Security of the University compound where Gung and group were situated was handled by Pakistani and Bangladeshi troops under the UN command.

Somali intra clan firefights broke out almost daily between rival warlords Aideed of the Habr Gedr clan and Ali Mahdi of the Abgal clan. Fortunately very little was aimed at Gung's compound and they only received sporadic incoming. These occurrences were probably due to excessive chewing of the drug "qat' or simply boredom of the heavily armed clansmen. After all much of the clans resources were obtained by stealing from or bribing of UN personnel.

Even though the conditions were Spartan, the Ambassador and the DCM were always dressed in coat and tie to enhance the US image. On the other hand Gung's intell crew customarily wore shorts, a tee shirt and a Browning 9mm at the hip. The uniform gave them the natural cover of a Brown & Root contractor and did not draw attention to their activities. USLO and Gung's intel crew were withdrawn to Nairobi on two occasions due to the poor security situation.

US policy was to convince the UN to withdraw all personnel and operations from Somalia. Gung, his commo man and his eight man military team were finally reinserted into Mogadishu to plan the withdrawal of all UN forces. Why did this planning fall on Gung's shoulders? The simple answer was that the UN had no capability to withdraw troops in a hostile environment. There existed the distinct possibility that the Somali clans would descend upon them like jackals to make an easy kill and steal supplies.

As the UN troops were withdrawn, the perimeter around the airport and seaport grew smaller. It was down to 100 meters in some areas. At this point, no admin withdrawal was feasible and a Battalion of US Marines and 500 special unit Italian troops were landed to secure a tight perimeter of less than 200 meters around the beach lines. At that point the remaining Pakistani troops withdrew through Marine lines and then it was a total US show.

That was a fun time for Gung as a former Marine. Other than the senior officers and the Sgt. Major, no one knew who the old bearded guy wearing shorts and a tee shirt was. Gung would check their lines and find places where he could meet his Somali assets. He would always get the questions, "who are you and what do you want?" Gung would answer, "I'm the old intel guy who has been here a year. If you have any other questions ask LtGen. Zinni, your battalion commander, or the Sgt. Major."After two more days of fun, Gung and his crew exfiled over the beach on a hydrofoil landing craft to the Amphibian vessel, "Belleau Wood." Several days later Gung embarked in Mombasa, his one year mission competed.

While on board ship Gung reflected on Somalia and his 30 year career, he thought it was time to retire and let the next generation enjoy the good times. Gung's career began as a young lieutenant platoon leader in the Corps in Viet Nam. It ended with his evacuation over the beach in Mogadishu with Marines. With a satisfied smile, Gung said, "It doesn't get much better than that."

⌒⌒⌒⌒

There was a war going on in Vietnam and the Viet Cong were getting supplied through Laos. At some point in time, the State Department decided to fight wars with a politically correct flavor. An indistinct policy that continues today, by not allowing our soldiers and marines to pursue the enemy across borders. This inept policy allowed the enemy to rely on sanctuaries that should not have been afforded to them.

Somewhere there was one government agency that still had the power in the 1960's to harass and discourage the enemy hiding in these sanctuaries. Paul was involved with training the Hmong in the use of modern weapons. They were used to crossbows and spears. Paul trained them to use automatic weapons. The only kind he could get was from World War II but they were more effective than their Stone Age weapons.

Gung conducted numerous successful raids and ambushes on the Pathet Lao and Viet Cong. He organized a resupply system through air drops in specific continually changing locations. This brave group of men, led by a brave United States intelligence agency, was effective in inhibiting the enemy.

Sadly, the State Department and short sighted bureaucrats in our government were able to end this effective system of counter-guerilla warfare we were using. When the politically liberal philosophy won out, the Hmong tribesmen were abandoned were eventually wiped out by the communist forces.

Today these liberals are successful in inhibiting our military in Afghanistan with a policy of ridiculously enacted, "rules of engagement." Our warriors cannot fight as soldiers fought since the beginning of time. That is, to close with, kill or capture the enemy. If these wimp factor politicians had their way, our military would be transformed into a social welfare agency.

It seems to this writer that the CIA has been vilified, maligned, disparaged and harassed more from our own politically correct politicians than from the enemy.

It is a sad story. But, thankfully due to Gung, Bag and many other brave patriots like them, our governments was able to hold back the expansion of communist forces during the cold war. Oh, yeah, we were successful in that cold war.

Gung went on to be active in many more wars. His talents were used in Central America, Africa and Europe during the Balkans war.

With regard to our military reserve regulations, it is an injustice that Gung came up on the short end. It is an inequity for a military man who engaged in combat engagements in five wars around the globe and then be dropped from the military reserve forces because he was unable to attend monthly meetings. It seems there should be a system for crediting these soldiers for their war experience. They should be allowed the same compensation reservists get upon retirement.

CHAPTER **21**

Looking Back

The memories from which this book is based began generations ago, long before I was born. There are roots in Russia, although I have no contact there with any family member, nor did my Dad. My Sicilian connections are far more extensive. I have cousins here who have done extensive research into the Livoti/Simone families. Many of my cousins have visited Sicily and some, including my parents, have visited the home town of Mazzera San Andrea.

As a document into the past, there exists Dad's biography, *The Way it Was, From Second Avenue to Staten Island,* Xlibris, 2005. This serves to chronicle, first hand, events in his and Mom's lives. Dad's book gives an insight into the hardships of tenement living in the Lower East Side of New York City. It shows the fears of a young boy who lost his mother at an early age.

Dad illustrates the kindness of his public school teachers and the warmth of his tenement dwelling neighbors for an orphan boy. Dad then describes the difficulties of finding work during the Great Depression and method of socializing they participated in. It was at a storefront club party that he met Mom.

In addition, there are the numerous sessions I had with Mom as she explained her family's saga. Then there are the magnificent memories that began in the summer of 1978 that are imbedded in my mind. The high altitude connection was furthered with reconnecting my friendship with Chuck Jensen.

There were many enjoyable hours spent with Arlene's son, Jeff Donlan. Those hours included hiking the mountain trails around Salida, venturing into caves whose walls were covered with swallow nests, and exploring the ghost town of St Elmo, CO. Jeff also took me to Turret, an abandoned mining town east of Salida where mines, hand dug in the 1800's, and they still exist.

Jeff I spent many pleasurable hours bicycle touring. The two of us did a century ride from Salida to Pueblo. A century is a 100 kilometer or 100 mile or bike ride. We didn't quite complete the century ride because Becky picked us up on the outskirts of Pueblo. I was so totally fatigued! Becky, in her dual rear wheeled pickup truck never looked more beautiful to me than anyone I had ever encountered in my life. Ugh, that was a brutal six hours for me. I was relieved to throw my bicycle into the bed of her pickup. I don't think Jeff ever got fatigued in any or our adventures.

There were summers when I transported both my Trek 1000 aluminum road bike and my Trek Mountain bike. Thanks to Jeff, they were both well used. I am forever grateful for his company and friendship. On our last trip, we were transported to the top of Monarch Mountain and we then began our downhill ride back to Poncha Springs via O'Haver Lake.

That 20-mile ride, though mostly downhill, was typically on a single track trail. I learned that single track was something to be respected, for me sometimes feared. Sometimes these trails were mere inches wide often just twice the width of the tires. Occasionally it was carved out of a mountainside where one of my shoulders was inches from the uphill side of the mountain and the other side fell away into a cliff. My first single track wipeout occurred on the Rainbow Trail above Salida, and I tumbled downhill. Thankfully, I was slowed down by brush and small trees but maintained my contact with my seat. I rode with Emillo Malquisa Juan Garcia, aka Mel, a friend of Jeff. He enthusiastically complimented me on my "technique." "Technique," I said, "I was just holding on." Apparently, I had done two 360 degree rolls and ended still in the bicycle seat and in an upright position.

On the ride with Jeff down from Monarch Mountain 20 miles West of Salida, I didn't have such a distinguished landing. My bike ended up in a boulder field with me maintaining fine technique, still attached to the bicycle seat. As I lay there looking up at the sky, all I could think of was where would the rescue helicopter land. I was certain I was hospital-bound. Jeff, who was ahead of me returned to ask if I was ok. As he helped me climb back on to the trail and realized the only thing broken was my helmet, I told him I was disappointed I would have to negotiate the rest of the trail and not wait for the arrival of a rescue helicopter. He assured me the trail got to be more reasonable ahead. As Always, Jeff was right. The remainder of the ride was a pleasure. It took us through Marshal Pass. We rolled past Mount Ouray and past O'Haver Lake. This ride Jeff selected displayed some of the most beautifully arrayed

Mt. Ouray and O'Haver Lake

vistas amid a measureless sea of beauty. We then rolled on into Poncha Springs where Jeff had his car parked.

As the librarian of the Salida Regional Library, Jeff had his finger on the pulse of this beautiful community. He always knew the best locations to ride, hike or camp. He is a great friend.

〰〰〰

This odyssey began with a lonely, worried man, wondering what the future had in store for him and his children. He was searching for a new identity because his previous one was shattered. It was shattered when his marriage with Irene ended. The role developed after 15 years of being a husband and father had to be replaced. It was that 1978 connection with Roy and Stu and the bonding between father and son that cemented a confidence for the man that would carry him for the rest of his life.

The following year, 1979, Debbie would accompany us. And still later in the 1990s, when I became reacquainted with Chuck, Nancy, Betsy, Debbie and Alex would fly out to the ranch in Salida where we would share delightful adventures together.

My hope is that the readers of this book, especially my grandchildren and their offspring, experience these exciting adventures as we did. Although the present technical and digital world has brought us unimaginable effects, there is no substitute for natural beauty and friendship. To be at a high altitude, in a pine forest region, with its fragrances and sounds is such a delight. It stays with one for a lifetime and maybe beyond.

Toward the Next Odyssey

CPSIA information can be obtained at www.ICGtesting.com
Printed in the USA
BVOW03s0942291113

337565BV00009B/150/P

9 781432 766696